“十三五”全国高等院校民航服务专业规划教材

民航英语阅读

主　编◎王　晶
副主编◎田　宇　吴立杰
编　委◎冯　维　闫　品　姜　舒

Civil Aviation English Reading

清华大学出版社
北　京

内 容 简 介

《民航英语阅读》是一本以提高民航空乘、飞行人员专业语言技能为主要任务的实用型专业教材。本书主要选取英美原版航空科技书籍的相关内容进行改编重写，并结合网络资源，取材具有一定的代表性、时效性和实用性。本书编者期望通过理论与实践相结合的方式，使读者做好航空语言和相关基础知识的储备。本书共分 18 课，内容均属航空公司的日常业务，包括航务、乘务、空中交通管制、通信导航、座舱设计、飞机维修、气象、紧急措施、人员训练和机场保安等各个方面。每课除课文、单词、常用词组、缩略语、注释、练习外，还附有阅读材料。书后附有 18 课课文的参考译文、航空英语扩展词汇和常用航空英语缩略语，以备考查。

本书将对今后研究各种英文阅读教材、探索具有中国民航特色的新时代英语阅读教材提供借鉴和指导。

图书在版编目（CIP）数据

民航英语阅读 / 王晶主编. —北京：清华大学出版社，2019（2024.7重印）
“十三五”全国高等院校民航服务专业规划教材
ISBN 978-7-302-52208-9

Ⅰ. ①民… Ⅱ. ①王… Ⅲ. ①民用航空-英语-阅读教学-高等职业教育-教材 Ⅳ. ①F56

中国版本图书馆CIP数据核字（2019）第016895号

责任编辑： 杜春杰
封面设计： 刘 超
版式设计： 文森时代
责任校对： 马军令
责任印制： 宋 林

出版发行： 清华大学出版社
网 址：https://www.tup.com.cn，https://www.wqxuetang.com
地 址：北京清华大学学研大厦 A 座 邮 编：100084
社 总 机：010-83470000 邮 购：010-62786544
投稿与读者服务：010-62776969，c-service@tup.tsinghua.edu.cn
质量反馈：010-62772015，zhiliang@tup.tsinghua.edu.cn
印 装 者： 涿州市般润文化传播有限公司
经 销： 全国新华书店
开 本： 185mm×260mm **印 张：** 13.5 **字 数：** 310 千字
版 次： 2019 年 10 月第 1 版 **印 次：** 2024 年 7 月第 2 次印刷
定 价： 49.80 元

产品编号：081526-01

“十三五”全国高等院校民航服务专业规划教材
丛书主编及专家指导委员会

丛书总主编 刘　永（北京中航未来科技集团有限公司董事长兼总裁）
丛书副总主编 马晓伟（北京中航未来科技集团有限公司常务副总裁）
丛书副总主编 郑大地（北京中航未来科技集团有限公司教学副总裁）
丛书总主审 朱益民（原海南航空公司总裁、原中国货运航空公司总裁、原上海航空公司总裁）
丛书英语总主审 王　朔（美国雪城大学、纽约市立大学巴鲁克学院双硕士）
丛书总顾问 沈泽江（原中国民用航空华东管理局局长）
丛书总执行主编 王益友［江苏民航职业技术学院（筹）院长、教授］
丛书艺术总顾问 万峻池（美术评论家、著名美术品收藏家）
丛书总航空法律顾问 程　颖（荷兰莱顿大学国际法研究生、全国高职高专“十二五”规划教材《航空法规》主审、中国东方航空股份有限公司法律顾问）

丛书专家指导委员会主任

关云飞（长沙航空职业技术学院教授）
张树生（国务院津贴获得者，山东交通学院教授）
刘岩松（沈阳航空航天大学教授）
宋兆宽（河北传媒学院教授）
姚　宝（上海外国语大学教授）
李剑峰（山东大学教授）
孙福万（国家开放大学教授）
张　威（沈阳师范大学教授）
成积春（曲阜师范大学教授）

“十三五”全国高等院校民航服务专业规划教材编委会

出 版 说 明

随着经济的稳步发展，我国已经进入经济新常态的阶段，特别是十九大指出：中国社会主要矛盾已经转化为人民日益增长的美好生活需要和不平衡不充分的发展之间的矛盾，这客观上要求社会服务系统要完善升级。作为公共交通运输的主要组成部分，民航运输在满足人们对美好生活的追求和促进国民经济发展中扮演着重要的角色，具有广阔的发展空间。特别是“十三五”期间，国家高度重视民航业的发展，将民航业作为推动我国经济社会发展的重要战略产业，预示着我国民航业将会有更好、更快的发展。从国产化飞机 C919 的试飞，到宽体飞机规划的出台，以及民航发展战略的实施，标志着我国民航业已经步入崭新的发展阶段，这一阶段的特点是以人才为核心，而这一发展模式必将进一步对民航人才质量提出更高的要求。面对民航业发展对人才培养提出的挑战，培养服务于民航业发展的高质量人才，不仅需要转变人才培养观念，创新教育模式，更需要加强人才培养过程中基本环节的建设，而教材建设就是其首要的任务。

我国民航服务专业的学历教育，经过 18 年的探索与发展，其办学水平、办学结构、办学规模、办学条件和师资队伍等方面都发生了巨大的变化，专业建设水平稳步提高，适应民航发展的人才培养体系初步形成。但我们应该清醒地看到，目前我国民航服务类专业的人才培养仍存在着诸多问题，特别是专业人才培养质量仍不能适应民航发展对人才的需求，人才培养的规模与高质量人才短缺的矛盾仍很突出。而目前相关专业教材的开发还处于探索阶段，缺乏系统性与规范性。已出版的民航服务类专业教材，在吸收民航服务类专业研究成果方面做出了有益的尝试，涌现出不同层次的系列教材，推动了民航服务的专业建设与人才培养，但从总体来看，民航服务类教材的建设仍落后于民航业对专业人才培养的实践要求，教材建设已成为相关人才培养的瓶颈。这就需要以引领和服务专业发展为宗旨，系统总结民航服务实践经验与教学研究成果，开发全面反映民航服务职业特点、符合人才培养规律和满足教学需要的系统性专业教材，积极有效地推进民航服务专业人才的培养工作。

基于上述思考，编委会经过两年多的实际调研与反复论证，在广泛征询民航业内专家的意见与建议、总结我国民航服务类专业教育的研究成果后，结合我国民航服务业的发展趋势，致力于编写出一套系统的、具有一定权威性和实用性的民航服务类系列教材，为推进我国民航服务人才的培养尽微薄之力。

本系列教材由沈阳航空航天大学、南昌航空大学、郑州航空工业管理学院、上海民航职业技术学院、长沙航空职业技术学院、西安航空职业技术学院、中原工学院、上海外国语大学、山东大学、大连外国语大学、沈阳师范大学、曲阜师范大学、湖南艺术职业学院、陕西师范大学、兰州大学、云南大学、四川大学、湖南民族职业学院、江西青年职业学院、天津交通职业学院、潍坊职业学院、南京旅游职业学院等多所高校的众多资深专家和学者共同打造，还邀请了多名原中国东方航空公司、原中国南方航空公司、原中国国际航空公司和原海南航空公司中从事多年乘务工作的乘务长和乘务员参与教材的编写。

目前，我国民航服务类的专业教育呈现着多元化、多层次的办学格局，各类学校的办学模式也呈现出个性化的特点，在人才培养体系、课程设置以及课程内容等方面，各学校之间存在着一定的差异，对教材也有不同的需求。为了能够更好地满足不同办学层次、教学模式对教材的需要，本套教材主要突出以下特点。

第一，兼顾本、专科不同培养层次的教学需要。鉴于近些年我国本科层次民航服务专业办学规模的不断扩大，在教材需求方面显得十分迫切，同时，专科层面的办学已经到了规模化的阶段，完善与更新教材体系和内容迫在眉睫，本套教材充分考虑了各类办学层次的需要，本着“求同存异、个性单列、内容升级”的原则，通过教材体系的科学架构和教材内容的层次化，以达到兼顾民航服务类本、专科不同层次教学之需要。

第二，将最新实践经验和专业研究成果融入教材。服务类人才培养是系统性问题，具有很强的内在规定性，民航服务的实践经验和专业建设成果是教材的基础，本套教材以丰富理论、培养技能为主，力求夯实服务基础、培养服务职业素质，将实践层面行之有效的经验与民航服务类人才培养规律的研究成果有效融合，以提高教材对人才培养的有效性。

第三，落实素质教育理念，注重服务人才培养。习近平总书记在党的十九大报告中强调，“要全面贯彻党的教育方针，落实立德树人根本任务，发展素质教育，推进教育公平，培养德智体美全面发展的社会主义建设者和接班人”，人才以德为先，以社会主义价值观铸就人的灵魂，才能使人才担当重任，也是高校人才培养的基本任务。教育实践表明，素质是人才培养的基础，也是人才职业发展的基石，人才的能力与技能以精神与灵魂为附着，但在传统的民航服务教材体系中，包含素质教育板块的教材较为少见。根据党的教育方针，本套教材的编写考虑到素质教育与专业能力培养的关系，以及素质对职业生涯的潜在影响，首次在我国民航服务专业教学中提出专业教育与人文素质并重、素质决定能力的培养理念，以独特的视野，精心打造素质教育教材板块，使教材体系更加系统，强化了教材特色。

第四，必要的服务理论与专业能力培养并重。调研分析表明，忽视服务理论与人文素质所培养出的人才很难有宽阔的职业胸怀与职业精神，其未来的职业生涯发展就会乏力。因此，教材不应仅是对单纯技能的阐述与训练指导，更应该是不淡化专业能力培养的同时，强化行业知识、职业情感、服务机理、职业道德等关系到职业发展潜力的要素的培养，以期培养出高层次和高质量的民航服务人才。

第五，架构适合未来发展需要的课程体系与内容。民航服务具有很强的国际化特点，而我国民航服务的思想、模式与方法也正处于不断创新的阶段，紧紧把握未来民航服务的发展趋势，提出面向未来的解决问题的方案，是本套教材的基本出发点和应该承担的责任。我们力图将未来民航服务的发展趋势、服务思想、服务模式创新、服务理论体系以及服务管理等内容进行重新架构，以期能对我国民航服务人才培养，乃至整个民航服务业的发展起到引领作用。

第六，扩大教材的种类，使教材的选择更加宽泛。鉴于我国目前尚缺乏民航服务专业更高层次办学模式的规范，各学校的人才培养方案各具特点，差异明显，为了使教材更适合于办学的需要，本套教材打破了传统教材的格局，通过课程分割、内容优化和课外外延化等方式，增加了教材体系的课程覆盖面，使不同办学层次、关联专业，可以通过教材合理组合获得完整的专业教材选择机会。

本套教材规划出版品种大约为四十种，分为：① 人文素养类教材，包括《大学语文》《应用文写作》《艺术素养》《跨文化沟通》《民航职业修养》《中国传统文化》等。② 语言类教材，包括《民航客舱服务英语教程》《民航客舱实用英语口语教程》《民航实用英语听力教程》《民航播音训练》《机上广播英语》《民航服务沟通技巧》等。③ 专业类教材，包括《民航概论》《民航服务概论》《中国民航常飞客源国概况》《民航危险品运输》《客舱安全管理与应急处置》《民航安全检查技术》《民航服务心理学》《航空运输地理》《民航服务法律实务与案例教程》等。④ 职业形象类教材，包括《空乘人员形体与仪态》《空乘人员职业形象设计与化妆》《民航体能训练》等。⑤ 专业特色类教材，包括《民航服务手语训练》《空乘服务专业导论》《空乘人员求职应聘面试指南》《民航面试英语教程》等。

为了开发职业能力，编者联合有关 VR 开发公司开发了一些与教材配套的手机移动端 VR 互动资源，学生可以利用这些资源体验真实场景。

本套教材是迄今为止民航服务类专业较为完整的教材系列之一，希望能借此为我国民航服务人才的培养，乃至我国民航服务水平的提高贡献力量。民航发展方兴未艾，民航教育任重道远，为民航服务事业发展培养高质量的人才是各类人才培养部门的共同责任，相信集民航教育的业内学者、专家之共同智慧，凝聚有识之士心血的这套教材的出版，对加速我国民航服务专业建设、完善人才培养模式、优化课程体系、丰富教学内容，以及加强师资队伍建设能起到一定的推动作用。在教材使用的过程中，我们真诚地希望听到业内专家、学者批评的声音，收到广大师生的反馈意见，以利于进一步提高教材的水平。

丛书序

《礼记·学记》曰："古之王者，建国君民，教学为先。"教育是兴国安邦之本，决定着人类的今天，也决定着人类的未来，企业发展也大同小异，重视人才是企业的成功之道，别无二选。航空经济是现代经济发展的新趋势，是当今世界经济发展的新引擎，民航是经济全球化的主流形态和主导模式，是区域经济发展和产业升级的驱动力。作为发展中的中国民航业，有巨大的发展潜力，其民航发展战略的实施必将成为我国未来经济发展的增长点。

"十三五"期间正值实现我国民航强国战略构想的关键时期，"一带一路"倡议方兴未艾，"空中丝路"越来越宽阔。面对高速发展的民航运输，需要推动持续的创新与变革；同时，基于民航运输的安全性和规范性的特点，其对人才有着近乎苛刻的要求，只有人才培养先行，夯实人才基础，才能抓住国家战略转型与产业升级的巨大机遇，实现民航运输发展的战略目标。经历多年民航服务人才发展的积累，我国建立了较为完善的民航服务人才培养体系，培养了大量服务民航发展的各类人才，保证了我国民航运输业的高速持续发展。与此同时，我国民航人才培养正面临新的挑战，既要通过教育创新，提升人才品质，又需要在人才培养过程中精细化，把人才培养目标落实到人才培养的过程中，而教材作为专业人才培养的基础，需要先行，从而发挥引领作用。教材建设发挥的作用并不局限于专业教育本身，其对行业发展的引领，专业人才的培养方向，人才素质、知识、能力结构的塑造以及职业发展潜力的培养具有不可替代的作用。

我国民航运输发展的实践表明，人才培养决定着民航发展的水平，而民航人才的培养需要社会各方面的共同努力。我们惊喜地看到，清华大学出版社秉承"自强不息，厚德载物"的人文精神，发挥强势的品牌优势，投身到民航服务专业系列教材的开发行列，改变了民航服务教材研发的格局，体现了其对社会责任的担当。

本套教材体系组织严谨，精心策划，高屋建瓴，深入浅出，具有突出的特色。第一，从民航服务人才培养的全局出发，关注了民航服务产业的未来发展趋势，架构了以培养目标为导向的教材体系与内容结构，比较全面地反映了服务人才培养趋势，具有良好的统领性；第二，很好地回归了教材的本质——适用性，体现在每本教材均有独特的视角和编写立意，既有高度的提升、理论的升华，也注重教育要素在课程体系中的细化，具有较强的可用性；第三，引入了职业素质教育的理念，补齐了服务人才素质教育缺少教材的短板，可谓是对传统服务人才培养理念的一次冲击；第四，教材编写人员参与面非常广泛。这反映出本套教材充分体现了当今民航服务专业教育的教学成果和编写者的思考，形成了相互交流的良性机制，势必对全国民航服务类专业的发展起到推动作用。

教材建设是专业人才培养的基础，与其服务的行业的发展交互作用，共同实现人才培养—社会检验的良性循环是助推民航服务人才的动力。希望这套教材能够在民航服务类专业人才培养的实践中，发挥更广泛的积极作用。相信通过不断总结与完善，这套教材一定会成为具有自身特色的、适应我国民航业发展要求的，以及深受读者喜欢的规范教材。

此为序。

原海南航空公司总裁、原中国货运航空公司总裁、原上海航空公司总裁

朱益民

2017 年 9 月

前　言

近年来随着世界空运业的迅速发展，以及我国民航在国际、国内业务的不断增加，越来越多的民航工作人员提出了学习民航服务专业英语的迫切愿望。为了更好地开展民航服务，提高民航工作人员的外语能力，为中国民航飞遍世界做出贡献，我们特意编写了这本《民航英语阅读》。

《民航英语阅读》是根据国际民航组织对乘务员、飞行员英语语言能力要求，结合国内航空公司对于乘务员、飞行员英语水平的要求和实际工作、训练需要而形成的具有飞行特色和时代特色的专业英语阅读教材。本教材融汇了国内现行大学英语阅读教材、其他文科教材和其他英语阅读教材的编写理念和模式，旨在帮助民航空中乘务、飞行技术、交通运输等专业的学生奠定民航英语基础知识，培养学生的民航英语综合应用能力。本教材从四个方面（语言、结构、词汇、理解）对学生进行语言能力的培养，有助于学生掌握专业知识、提高应用能力。本教材的编写全面贯彻国际民航组织的新语言标准。

《民航英语阅读》在选材上立足于空中乘务专业、飞行技术专业、交通运输专业的学生及航空公司工作人员等英语学习者的专业英语学习阶段的语言基础和专业英语基础语言知识学习的需要。本教材强调“以学生自主学习为中心，教师适时引导”的教学原则，在选材上注重基础性、实用性、全面性、系统性和前瞻性。每课的内容自成体系，取材具有典型性，每课力求专业英语知识的系统性，以引导读者在课外进行相关英语语言知识的学习。每课包括 Text 和 Supplementary Reading Material 两个部分。Text 包括 Passage、New words、Phrases and expressions、Notes、Exercises 几个部分。这种构建形式有别于国内其他阅读教材的单一性，其形式和内容以民航飞行英语涉及内容的特点为基础。Supplementary Reading Material 便于学习者课外学习，是对课文内容的补充和完善。

本教材是国内专门提高空中乘务及飞行技术等专业大学生及空运业（含空军）人员英语阅读能力的教材。《民航英语阅读》标志着国内民航乘务员、飞行员专业英语阅读教学迈出了探索特色课程建设重要一步。

编　者

2018 年 9 月

CONTENTS 目录

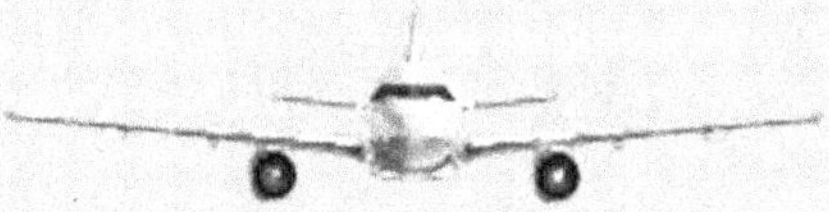

Unit One

A Brief Introduction to Modern Airplanes

Text

Passage

In contemporary society, airplane has become one of the most important means of transportation. Despite the different types, aircrafts, manufactured by different companies in aviation industry, share many standard features in common. Propeller aircrafts are still used by some small airlines, especially for regional transportation and in general aviation. However, international airlines use jet planes nearly on all of their flights.

Airplanes of different types may vary in their size, configuration, capacity, performance and so on. And they are usually identified by the manufacturer in combination with a series of model number. For instance, the Boeing 707, the first commercially successful jet airliner, is a medium sized, long-range narrow-body jet airliner with four engines. Versions of the aircraft have a capacity from 140 to 219 passengers and a range of 2,500 to 5,750 nautical miles. Its cruising speed is 470 tts and its maximum operating range is 5,757 miles. It flies at an average altitude of 25,000 to 40,000 feet. There are two galley complexes for first-class and economy passengers respectively. Besides, there are two auxiliary galleys on board. The lounge for the first-class passengers is located in the forward part of the aircraft.

Compared with the 707, Boeing 727 is smaller and is mainly intended for short and medium-length flights. It can carry 149 to 189 passengers and later model can fly up to 2,700 nautical miles nonstop. It has three engines, one on each side of the rear fuselage with a center engine attached to the base of the fin. It is Boeing's only trijet aircraft. It cruises at a speed of 575 miles per hour at altitudes from 25,000 to 42,000 feet. There is one galley and a service bar as well as some small working areas on board.

Among all jet planes made by Boeing, the 747 is the largest and is often referred to by its original nickname, "Jumbo Jet". Most airlines dislike the name since it implies clumsiness. The Boeing 747 is a wide-body commercial jet airliner and cargo aircraft with four engines and its distinctive hump-like upper deck along the forward part of the aircraft makes it among the world's most recognizable aircraft. The specially-designed deck is to serve as a first class lounge or extra seating or allows the aircraft to be easily converted to a cargo carrier by removing seats and installing a front cargo door. Aircraft of this type can accommodate 366 passengers in a normal configuration. But if converted into all-economy configuration, it can carry up to 490 passengers. First flown commercially in 1970, the 747 held the passenger capacity record for 37 years. The 747-400, the most common variant in service, has a high subsonic cruise speed up to 570 mph with an intercontinental range of 7,260 nautical miles. There are six galleys, three auxiliary galleys and twelve lavatories on Boeing 747. Some airlines have improved the interior of the plane so that the passengers could enjoy greater luxury and comfort.

Apart from the Boeing series, other popular American aircraft include McDonnell Douglas DC-8 and DC-10 as well as the Lockheed Tristar 1011. Another giant in the filed of airplane manufacturing is Airbus, which is a European multinational corporation. It produces and markets the first commercially viable digital fly-by-wire airliner, like the A320 and A340. And the A380 is the world's largest passenger airliner.

As for medium and long-range airplanes, the fuselage is composed of two main sections, the flight deck or the cockpit where the pilot and other flight crew work, and the cabin where the passengers stay. The cabin can be further divided into first class cabin in the forward part and the economy class in the rear part. There is a bulkhead between the two sections which can be moved forward or backward to adjust the number of seats for each class on a certain flight. The flight deck is separated from the cabin by another bulkhead. The partition between the cabin and the galley is also called bulkhead.

Generally speaking, there are more seats in economy class cabin than in first class cabin except on some special occasions such as charters. The first class section is the class with the best service, and is typically the highest priced. It is characterized by having a larger amount of space between seats, some of which can even be converted into beds, high quality food and drinks, personalized service and so on. Economy class seats are much cheaper than those of first class simply because the level of comfort is lower. The distance between each seat is short, and there is a smaller variety of food and entertainment. There is also business class cabin which is superior to the economy class while inferior to the first class.

Passenger capacity varies with the seat configuration chose by the operating airline. Airline cabins are frequently classified as narrow-body if there is a single aisle with seats on either side like Airbus A320 family and Boeing 737 or wide-body if there are two aisles with a block of seats between them in addition to the seats on the side, such as the Boeing 747 or the Airbus A380. Usually, a seating chart or aircraft seat map will be published for informational purposes or for the passengers to select their seats at booking or check-in, which indicates the basic seating layout, the numbering and lettering of the seats, the location of the emergency exits, lavatories, galleys, bulkheads and wings. There is a seating chart with the passengers' names for the convenience of the flight service crew as well as for record-keeping. The seats on board are marked with letters and numbers. In many planes, the letters begin with "A" on the left side of the cabin, with the highest letter on the rightmost side. Occasionally, the terms "port" and "starboard", which are borrowed from nautical terms originally, are also used to refer to left and right respectively. People also use the words "inboard" and "outboard" to indicate the location of the seats compared with the window or aisle. Inboard means the seats are closest to the aisle, while outboard implies that the seats are closest to the window. For medium-sized and small aircrafts, the numbers of the seats usually begin with "one" at the front part for first class and at the rear part for economy. And the largest number will appear at the bulkhead that separates the two sections. Some airlines may mark seats with the names of passengers in first class cabin.

New words

1. transportation [trænspɔːˈteɪʃ(ə)n]	n.	运输
2. manufacture [mænjʊˈfæktʃə]	v.	制造，加工
3. propeller [prəˈpelə]	n.	螺旋桨，推进器
4. configuration [kənˌfɪgəˈreɪʃ(ə)n]	n.	结构，布局，配置
5. altitude [ˈæltɪtjuːd]	n.	高度，海拔
6. galley [ˈgælɪ]	n.	船上的厨房
7. complex [ˈkɒmpleks]	n.	合成物，综合设施，复合体
8. auxiliary [ɔːgˈzɪljərɪ]	adj.	辅助的，从属的，附加的
9. lounge [laʊn(d)ʒ]	n.	休息室
10. nonstop [nɒnˈstɒp]	adv.	直达地，不停地
11. trijet [ˈtraɪdʒet]	n.	三喷气发动机飞机
12. clumsiness [ˈklʌmzɪnɪs]	n.	笨拙，丑陋
13. distinctive [dɪˈstɪŋ(k)tɪv]	adj.	有特色的，与众不同的
14. deck [dek]	n.	甲板，层面
15. convert [kənˈvɜːt]	v.	（使）转变
16. cargo [ˈkɑːgəʊ]	n.	货物，船货
17. subsonic [sʌbˈsɑnɪk]	adj.	亚音速的，比音速稍慢的
18. lavatory [ˈlævət(ə)rɪ]	n.	厕所，盥洗室
19. viable [ˈvaɪəbl]	adj.	可行的
20. fuselage [ˈfjuːzəlɑːʒ]	n.	（飞机）机身
21. rear [rɪə]	adj.	后面的
22. bulkhead [ˈbʌlkhed]	n.	（船，飞机的）舱壁
23. partition [pɑːˈtɪʃ(ə)n]	n.	隔板，隔墙
24. charter [ˈtʃɑːtə]	n.	包机
25. aisle [aɪl]	n.	过道，通道

Phrases and expressions

1. aviation industry	航空工业
2. general aviation	通用航空

3. medium-sized	中型的
4. long-range	远程
5. narrow-body	窄体
6. nautical mile	海里
7. cruising speed	巡航速度
8. operating range	航程
9. emergency exit	紧急出口
10. first class cabin	头等舱
11. economy class cabin	经济舱
12. business class cabin	商务舱

Notes

1. The Boeing 747 is a wide-body commercial jet airliner and cargo aircraft with four engines and its distinctive hump-like upper deck along the forward part of the aircraft makes it among the world's most recognizable aircraft.

波音 747 是一架宽体四发通用喷气式客货两用飞机。其独特的机身前部上层客舱隆起的造型使得它成为世界上最容易辨认的飞机。

2. Another giant in the filed of airplane manufacturing is Airbus, which is a European multinational corporation. The company produces and markets the first commercially viable digital fly-by-wire airliner, like the A320 and A340.

飞机制造业中的另一个巨头是空客。它是欧洲一家跨国公司。该公司生产并销售了第一架使用数字电传系统的商用客机，如 A320 和 A340。

3. As for medium and long-range airplanes, the fuselage is composed of two main sections, the flight deck or the cockpit where the pilot and other flight crew work, and the cabin where the passengers stay.

用于中程和远程飞行的飞机机身主要由两部分构成——飞行员和其他机组人员工作的驾驶舱和供乘客休息的客舱。

Exercises

I. Write down the full name of each abbreviation and translate it into Chinese.

1. CAAC
2. FAA
3. EASA
4. IATA
5. ICAO

6. PPL
7. CPL
8. ATPL
9. IR
10. CRM

II. Translate the following sentences into English.

1. 尽管飞机可以设计用于很多不同的目的，大多数飞机主要结构是相同的，包括机身、机翼、尾翼、起落架和发动机。

2. 机身是飞机上用来装载工作人员、乘客、货物、武器和机载设备的主要部分，它将飞机的各个部件连成一个整体。

3. 机翼为飞机提供主要的升力，升力在机翼与空气进行相对运动的过程中产生。

4. 飞行操纵面包括飞机上所有活动面，使飞行员可以调整和控制飞机的姿态。

5. 飞机尾翼包括固定的水平安定面和垂直安定面，维持飞机的稳定性。水平安定面防止机头上下晃动（俯仰），垂直安定面阻止机头左右晃动（偏航）。

III. Read and translate the following short passages into Chinese.

1. An aircraft is a machine that is able to fly by gaining support from the air. It counters the force of gravity by using either static lift or the dynamic lift of an airfoil, or in a few cases the downward thrust from jet engines. Common examples of aircraft include airplanes, helicopters, airships, gliders and hot air balloons. The human activity that surrounds aircraft is called aviation. Crewed aircraft is flown by an onboard pilot, but unmanned aerial vehicles may be remotely controlled or self-controlled by onboard computers.

2. C919 is China's first domestically produced single-aisle passenger jet manufactured by Commercial Aircraft Corporation of China (COMAC). The two-engine C919 is a sleek, modern and efficient airplane, mainly used for medium-haul flights with 158 seats. C919 made its maiden flight in Shanghai Pudong International Airport in 2017. The first flight of the C919 marks a major breakthrough for China's domestic civil aircraft industry, and the C919 could have the opportunity to break the monopolies of Boeing and Airbus.

IV. Answer the following questions according to the text.

1. What is the largest airplane in Boeing series? How much do you know about this aircraft?
2. What is the difference between first class cabin and economy class cabin?
3. What can be called a wide-body aircraft? What is a narrow-body aircraft?
4. What information may be printed on the aircraft seating chart?
5. How are the seats usually identified on a passenger plane?

Supplementary Reading Material

End of an era: United bids farewell to the Boeing 747
——Here's a look at the "Queen of the Skies"

A chapter of aviation history closes Tuesday when United Airlines bids farewell to the Boeing 747, the jumbo jet that made air travel way more affordable for millions of people around the globe.

The double-decker plane with the humped fuselage is one of the world's most recognized planes. But after flying the four-engine, fuel-guzzling plane for decades, United and other airlines are retiring the so-called Queen of the Skies in favor of sleeker, more cost-efficient models. The planes are used frequently for cargo, which was the reason for the plane's design. Some models were given a hinged nose to allow for easy loading of goods.

United's first 747 took off from San Francisco and flew to Honolulu in 1970. It's repeating that route for the final passenger flight Tuesday, complete with a crew dressed in 1970s uniforms. Smoking will not be permitted, however.

In a sign of how efficient modern planes have become, Southwest Airlines announced,it will offer service to Hawaii, and new, single-aisle Boeing 737 will likely do the job.

Delta Air Lines will retire its Boeing 747 fleet by January, the last U.S. airline to do so. But the plane will live on as a workhorse cargo jet, flown by UPS and others. Here's a look at the Boeing 747, and how it changed the world from its introduction nearly five decades ago:

A tall order

Joe Sutter, who died last year, led the engineering team that designed the Boeing 747 in the mid-1960s. It took 50,000 employees to bring the plane to life. Boeing says it took 29 months from "conception to rollout," which earned the team the nickname "The Incredibles". Below is a prototype of the jumbo jet in 1968.

Take off

The 747's first flight was in February 1969. It entered into commercial service in 1970. The plane was more than 231 feet long and its tail was taller than a six-story building.

Global jet set

Orders rolled in quickly from airlines, including PanAm and TWA. The airlines were eager for the glamour buy and to fill the large planes with thousands of members of the new jet set.

High-touch service

Air travel, even in the 1970s, was a luxury, and service aboard the 747 in the early days was elaborate compared with the no-frills era of modern air travel.

Service on both decks

Decades before Gulf carriers introduced their flashy cabins, posh lounges were the place to see and be seen in the 1970s. Frank Sinatra Jr. once performed in an American Airlines 747 lounge (with a piano) on a red-eye flight from Los Angeles to New York, an attempt to draw more passengers. The planes could fit some 500 people, and later, airlines got rid of the spacious upper-deck lounges and focused on fitting as many passengers as possible into the plane, which made travel more affordable but less comfortable.

Ferrying the Space Shuttle

NASA used modified Boeing 747s from 1974 for activities including the study of air turbulence from large aircraft to the more glamorous job of ferrying space shuttles like the Columbia.

Cargo is king

The hinged nose of the 747 cargo version allows for easy access to its cavernous interiors.

Shuttling presidents

Two Boeing 747-200Bs make up the Air Force One fleet. President Donald Trump late last year complained about the cost of the scheduled replacement of the jets, famously tweeting

"Cancel order"!

No US airline will operate a 747 by the end of the year

Delta is also retiring its Boeing 747 fleet this year, replacing the jumbo jets with the twin-engine Airbus A350 planes.

They will become rarer on foreign carriers, too

British Airways recently announced that it will retire its 747 fleet by 2024.

People still stare at "the Queen"

As the plane becomes a rarer sight at airports, passengers still often stop to get a look at the "Queen of the Skies."

资料来源：https://www.cnbc.com/2017/11/07/the-boeing-747-jumbo-jet-the-plane-that-changed-the-world.html

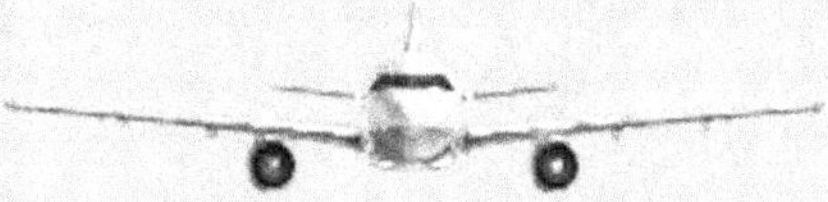

Unit Two
Supersonic Aircraft

Text

Passage

All current civil aircrafts, including airliners, helicopters and airships, as well as many military types, are subsonic, with a maximum speed less than the speed of sound. Most jet aircrafts cruise at a subsonic speed of 550 mph. They pass through the air and create a series of pressure waves in front of it and behind it, similar to the bow and stern waves created by a boat, however, this wave is spherical rather than ring-shaped.

At subsonic speed, the aircraft sends relatively small pressure differences to the front as an alarm signal for the air ahead, therefore the air molecules have time to get out of the way and flow smoothly around the wing and the tail.

Supersonic aircrafts are able to fly faster than the speed of sound, Mach 1 (around 660 mph at 50,000 feet), which are used almost entirely for research and military purposes. They cruise at the initial speed of a 0.303 rifle bullet. When the aircraft approaches the speed of sound, the alarm signals for the air ahead become shorter, giving the molecules less time to get out of the way. The compressed molecules form into a severer vertical shockwave as the aircraft reaches the speed of sound. Its pressure increases instantaneously, so in the vicinity of the source it sounds like the crackling bullwhip.

Once the aircraft speeds up over Mach 1, the shockwave forms a cone. As the apex of the cone, the aircraft drags it forward. Because only at the high altitude can supersonic flight be achieved, there is ample time for the shockwave to enlarge significantly before it gets to the ground. Finally, near the ground we hear a muffled rumble by the weakened shockwave. Nevertheless, people are worried about the possible consequences of supersonic flight，they complain that the shockwaves will damage human ears as well as buildings. As a matter of fact, there are two shockwaves in the cone, respectively from the nose and the tail, producing deep double boom or persistent air disturbance, sounding like thunder or the sound of explosions in the distance.

A supersonic transport (SST) is a civilian supersonic aircraft designed to transport passengers at speeds greater than the speed of sound. The airframe of a supersonic transport is streamlined, with a pointed nose and two thin delta wings extending from the nose to the tail. The aircraft's nose was designed as a so sharp shape that the air swirls over it to create a mighty vortex which gives increased lift during take off and landing. The cabin windows of SST are designed smaller so as to reduce the probability of in the highly pressurized cabin.

When the aircraft makes transonic acceleration, the passengers can hardly feel it, because the ground below seems to pass by at a normal speed looked down from the 50,000-feet supersonic cruising altitude, where clouds look far away below the aircraft and recognizable ground features are extremely small. It is a wonderful experience for the passengers of supersonic aircraft to see a fantastic scenery: the sky looks like a dark purple shade and the horizon is obviously curved.

To date, the only SSTs to see regular service have been Concorde and the Tupolev Tu-144. The last passenger flight of the Tu-144 was in June 1978 and it was last flown in 1999 by NASA. Concorde's last commercial flight was in October 2003, with a November 26, 2003 ferry flight being was its last airborne operation. Following the permanent cessation of flying by Concorde, there are no remaining SSTs in commercial service. Several companies have each proposed a supersonic business jet, which may bring supersonic transport back again.

New words

1. supersonic [ˌsu:pə'sɒnɪk]	adj. 超声波的，超音速的
2. helicopter ['helɪkɒptə(r)]	n. 直升飞机
3. spherical ['sferɪk(ə)l]	adj. 球形的，球面的；天体的，天空的
4. ring-shaped [rɪŋʃept]	adj. 环形的，环状的
5. molecule ['mɒlɪkju:l]	n. 分子，微小颗粒
6. rifle ['raɪfl]	n. 步枪；来福枪
7. vertical ['vɜ:tɪkl]	adj. 垂直的，竖立的
8. shockwave [ʃɔkwev]	n. 震荡波，冲击波
9. instantaneously [ˌɪnstən'teɪnɪəslɪ]	adv. 即刻，突如其来地
10. crackle ['krækl]	vi. 发出轻微的爆裂声，发出噼啪声
11. bullwhip ['bʊlwɪp]	n. 粗而长的鞭
12. Mach [mɑ:k]	n. 马赫，马赫数（速度单位，常用于计算飞行速度，马赫等于音速）
13. cone [kəʊn]	n. 圆锥体；球果；圆锥形
14. apex ['eɪpeks]	n. 顶点，最高点
15. muffle ['mʌfl]	vt. 发出低沉的声音；抑制
16. rumble ['rʌmbl]	n. 隆隆声
17. disturbance [dɪ'stɜ:b(ə)ns]	n. 困扰，打扰；骚乱，变乱；烦闷
18. airframe ['eəˌfreɪm]	n. 机身
19. streamlined ['stri:mlaɪnd]	adj.（汽车、飞机等）流线型的；改进的，最新型的
20. delta ['deltə]	n.（河流的）三角洲

21. swirl [swɜ:l] vi. 旋转，打旋
22. vortex ['vɔ:teks] n. 低涡，涡旋
23. pressurized ['preʃəraɪzd] adj. 加压的，增压的
24. acceleration [ək'sɛlə'reʃən] n. 加速，促进；加速度
25. horizon [hə'raɪzn] n. 地平线；范围；界限；眼界
26. curve [kɜ:v] n. 弧线，曲线
27. ferry ['feri] n. 渡船，摆渡，渡口
28. airborne ['eəbɔ:n] adj. 空运的，飞机载的；航空的
29. cessation [se'seɪʃn] n.（暂时）停止，休止，中断

Phrases and expressions

1. supersonic aircraft 超音速飞机
2. maximum speed 最大速度，全速
3. subsonic speed 亚音速
4. pressure wave 压力波
5. pressure difference 压力差
6. alarm signal 警报
7. air molecule 空气分子
8. initial speed 初速度
9. air disturbance 大气扰动
10. delta wing 三角翼
11. cruising altitude 巡航高度

Abbreviations

1. SST supersonic transport 超音速运输机
2. NASA National Aeronautics and Space Administration 美国国家航空航天局

Notes

1. They cruise at the initial speed of a 0.303 rifle bullet.

它们（超音速飞机）以 0.303 口径步枪子弹离膛的初始速度巡航。

2. The aircraft's nose was designed as a so sharp shape that the air swirls over it to create a mighty vortex which give increased lift during takeoff and landing.

飞机的机头被设计成一个非常锋利的形状，空气在它上面盘旋形成一个强大的涡流，在起飞和降落时增加升力。

3. To date, the two SSTs to see regular service have been Concorde and the Tupolev Tu-144.

到目前为止，可用于定期航行的超音速客机只有协和式飞机和图波列夫 Tu-144 飞机。

Exercises

I. Analyze the following passages grammatically.

1. They pass through the air and create a series of pressure waves in front of it and behind it, similar to the bow and stern waves created by a boat, however, this wave is spherical rather than ring-shaped.

2. When the aircraft makes transonic acceleration, the passengers can hardly feel it, because the ground below seems to pass by at a normal speed looked down from the 50,000-feet supersonic cruising altitude, where clouds look far away below the aircraft and recognizable ground features are extremely small.

II. Answer the following questions based on the text.

1. What will happen when the aircraft approaches the speed of sound?
2. What will happen once the aircraft speeds up over Mach1?
3. What is a supersonic transport?
4. Why do the cabin windows of SST are designed smaller?
5. Please list the names of supersonic transports that have been used for regular service.

Supplementary Reading Material

Things to Know About NASA's Supersonic X-Plane

NASA has announced plans to design and build an aircraft that can fly faster than the speed of sound with quiet, supersonic technology. The experimental plane, or X-plane, is called the Low-Boom Flight Demonstration (LBFD) and will be designed to reduce the sonic boom associated with supersonic flight, according to NASA's press release.

NASA has given Lockheed Martin a $247.5 million contract to build the unique, single-pilot plane by 2021. This marks the first time in decades the agency is moving forward with a piloted X-plane, according to the release.

Here's what you need to know about the super quiet, supersonic jet.

When was the first supersonic flight?

The first flight to break the sound barrier was the Bell X-1, which took to the skies in 1947 with Chuck Yeager as pilot. Yeager became the fastest man on Earth when he reached a speed of Mach 1.06, Jack Stewart reported for Wired last fall. Mach 1 is equal to the speed of sound in air, which varies depending on temperature and altitude (at 50 degrees Fahrenheit, it's about 754 miles per hour). In 1967, the X-15 set a manned speed record by flying at hypersonic speeds above Mach 5.

Why make a supersonic plane?

It's all about speed. The last commercial supersonic flight, Concorde, could travel from London to New York in less than three and a half hours, cruising at speeds of around 1,350 mph. Today, most airlines take closer to seven and a half hours to complete the same trip.

The travel benefits are clear, but there's still the issue of the noise associated with supersonic flight, known as a sonic boom. With this latest X-plane, one thing researchers are attempting to do is to reduce the noise.

What is sonic boom?

NASA has researched sonic booms since the 1940s. According to a NASA press release, shockwaves from traditional aircraft designs combine as they move away and expand from the airplane's nose and tail. This results into two roaring sonic booms.

While NASA's goal with its newest X-plane isn't to silence the sound, they're attempting to make it much softer. "I'm trying not to use the word sonic boom," Peter Coen, project manager for NASA's Commercial Supersonics Technology Project, tells Mashable's Mark Kaufman. "I'm trying to ban that from everyone's vocabulary."

What's unique about the newest X-plane?

The X-plane's design will include sleek features that will help it barely make a noise as it flies over cities. As Jack Stewart writes for Wired, the plane's long, pointy nose and "swept back wings" makes it look a little like a missile.

The design's shape minimizes the shockwaves and prevents them from colliding. Instead, it directs them to the ground still separated, the press release states. People on the ground should hear something like a car door closing rather than an epic boom.

And while it won't reach Concorde speeds just yet, the new X-plane is designed to fly at about 940 mph at an altitude of 55,000 feet. It will be the length of an NBA basketball court, LiveScience's Brandon Specktor writes.

Why is commercial supersonic flights not running today?

The era of commercial supersonic flights stretched from 1969 to 2003, Mark Ellwood reports for The Wall Street Journal. But noise and environmental concerns plagued the period. The era ended soon after the supersonic Concorde's tragic crash in 2000, BBC News reported. The number of passengers choosing to go supersonic never rebounded.

Since then, commercial supersonic flights over land have been banned. But if all goes as planned, the new X-plane could revolutionize air travel.

资料来源：https://www.smithsonianmag.com/smithsonianmag/five-things-know-about-nasas-newest-x-plane-180968685/

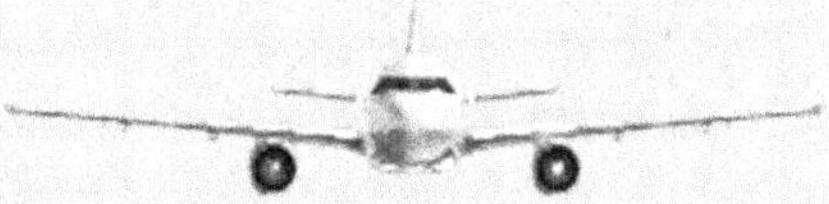

Unit Three
The Flight Deck

Text

Passage

Inside the flight deck there is calm. The engines can only just be heard and the sensation of movement comes mostly from the sound of air round the nose of the aircraft. Above the cloud layers, the view is far-ranging but dazzling, particularly when flying into the sun. At high altitudes, other aircrafts are hard to distinguish against the bright light and dark blue of the stratosphere.

The flight deck is designed to allow both pilots to reach all the essential controls and switches without moving from their seats. There may be more than 150 instruments, some with digital readouts, most with the familiar circular dial, but not all have to be watched at once. Pilots rarely concentrate on one particular instrument, but scan them all at intervals. Immediately in front of each pilot is the Basic T, aviation's standard arrangement of the four principal readings, showing speed, height, attitude and heading. The instruments are arranged so that the most important are closest to the pilot.

Aviation has its traditions. In the early years, influenced by the keepright rules of the road and at sea, aircraft also kept right on the airways. For ease of visibility captains chose to sit on the left.

All the primary instruments and controls are duplicated and for some there is even a third standby instrument. In the unlikely event of one of the pilots collapsing, the other has all the controls needed to fly safely. In flight, each pilot can monitor the other's instruments, and ensure that they are giving the same indications on both panels.

There is also a highly sophisticated centralized warning system on the main instrument panel. Red or yellow illuminated squares accompanied by loud buzzing indicate immediately any failure of any part of the aircraft and its control systems. The strident sound of any of 18 different warning signals could disturb the serenity of a flight deck.

All airlines may shortly adopt a feature at present only used in some civil airliners and military aircraft-electronic headup display (HUD). Height, speed and heading, and a picture of the runway, can be projected electronically onto the windshield so the pilot can look "head-up" to see the picture merging with the real runway during a landing approach. This system saves the essential two or three seconds the pilot loses in adjusting his vision from the instruments to the runway.

New words

1. sensation [sen'seiʃ(ə)n] n. 感觉，知觉，感动
2. layer ['leiə] n. 层
3. dazzle ['dæzl] v.（太阳光等）眩眼，耀眼
4. stratosphere ['strætəsfir] n. 平流层，同温层
5. digital ['didʒitl] adj. 数字的
6. circular ['sə:kjulə] adj. 圆形的，循环的
7. dial ['daiəl] n. 刻度盘，数字盘
8. scan [skæn] v. 扫描，搜索
9. interval ['intəv(ə)l] n. 间隔，间歇
10. attitude ['ætitju:d] n. 姿态，看法，意见
11. visibility [ˌvizi'biliti] n. 能见度，可见性
12. panel ['pænl] n. 面板，仪表板
13. sophisticate [sə'fistikeit] v. 使复杂，使精致
14. centralize ['sentrəlaiz] v. 形成中心，集中
15. illuminate [i'l(j)u:mineit] v. 照明，照亮
16. buzz [bʌz] v. 嗡嗡叫
17. strident ['straidnt] adj. 轧轧响的，刺耳的
18. serenity [si'reniti] n. 宁静，平静
19. adopt [ə'dɔpt] v. 采用，采纳
20. windshield ['win(d)ʃi:ld] n. 挡风（玻璃），风罩
21. merge [mɜ:dʒ] v. 合并，结合
22. approach [ə'prəutʃ] v. 接近，靠近
    n. 方法，途径，接近
23. vision ['viʒən] n. 视力，视觉

Phrases and expressions

1. cloud layers 云层
2. up to 直到，多达，胜任
3. digital readouts 数字式读数
4. at intervals 不时
5. in the event of 万一，如果
6. warning system 报警系统
7. main instrument panel 主仪表盘
8. control system 控制系统

Abbreviation

HUD headup display 平视显示；平视显示器

Notes

1. Inside the flight deck there is calm.
驾驶舱内一片寂静。

2. For ease of visibility captains chose to sit on the left.
为了便于观察，机长选择坐在左座上。

3. All airlines may shortly adopt a feature at present only used in some civil airlines and military aircraft ——electronic headup display.

所有的航空公司可能会很快采用目前只在某些民航班机和军用飞机上使用的装置——电子平视显示器。

Exercises

I. Identify the following components.

1. overhead switch panel
2. navigational radio selector
3. autopilot power switch
4. flap lever
5. landing-gear control handle
6. thrust levers
7. computer selection switch
8. centre console
9. rudder pedals
10. Automatic direction finder (ADF)

II. Explain these special terms with the help of the dictionary and learn by heart.

1. Instrument: Any device which shows visually or aurally the altitude, attitude, or operation of an aircraft or any part contained within an aircraft.

2. Visibility: The ability, as determined by atmospheric conditions and expressed in distance, to see and identify prominent unlighted objectives by day or night visibility is reported as statute miles, hundreds of feet or in meters.

3. Computerized: Equipped with a machine which electronically provides rapid solutions to simple or complex calculations.

III. Answer the following questions according to the text.

1. How is a flight deck designed? How many instruments are there in it?

2. Do pilots concentrate on one particular instrument?

3. What are the four principal readings?

4. What rules do aircraft keep on the airways according to aviation tradition? Which side do captains choose to sit?

5. What do the red or yellow illuminated squares indicate? What kind of feature may all airlines adopt in the future?

Supplementary Reading Material

Why the flight deck of an airplane is called a "cockpit"

Since the day I started to fly an airplane, the area where the pilots sit in front to control the plane has always being referred to as the "cockpit". Why it is often referred to as such is probably due to the fascination and uniqueness of this term. There are neither "cocks" nor "pits" around in the first place and yet the term is stuck to mean the flight deck of an airliner.

From the sources that I have researched, "cockpit" also comes from the rather barbaric sport of cockfighting and refers to the pit in which the fights occurred. Shortly thereafter, the word naturally attained a connotation as being related to any scene of grisly combat.

Let's have a look at an excerpt from word-detective.com:

The first "cockpits" were actual pits in the ground constructed (to the extent that one "constructs" a pit) to house "cockfights" to the death between game cocks (essentially very belligerent chickens). Cockfighting, a barbaric "sport" usually conducted for gambling purposes, probably originated in ancient China and remains distressingly popular around the world.

Well, this term is also used in relation to ships. "Cockpit" in the 1700s was referred to as the compartment below decks on a British naval vessel. The often cramped and confined compartment was placed below the waterline and served as quarters for junior officers as well as for treating the wounded during battle.

Here is another version of the explanation by another source from the Internet:

In the early days of aviation aircraft had open cockpits and the overhead of biplanes had wet wings. The petcock, which is usually a small spring loaded valve to control fuel flow from the tanks to the engine as well as to drain a sample of fuel from the tanks for contaminants such as water or grit that may inadvertently enter the fuel.

A person could drain off the water which is heavier than fuel. Water sinks to the lowest part of the tank-where the petcock is installed. The actual petcock on most early aircraft was where the wings came together at the center of the fuselage which was directly overhead the open seat of the pilot, making where the pilot sat as the pit under the petcock or "cockpit".

Even today, a room on the lower deck of a yacht or motor boat where the crew quarters are located is often called a "cockpit". In addition, the rudder control space from which a vessel is steered is sometimes called a "cockpit" since a watchman in the highest position is called a cock, and a cavity in any vessel is called a pit.

Just like how the word "knots" to measure the sailing speed as well as "port and starboard" (left and right) sides of a ship and amongst others, are also applied on airplanes. So "cockpit", as an often confined space used for control purposes, was also applied to aircraft around 1914 by pilots during World War I. In keeping with this same meaning, the tightly confined control space of a racing automobile has also became known as a cockpit by about 1935.

So, in the modern sense "cockpit" now includes the entire crew areas of large airliners, which are usually fairly spacious and not the scene of conflict.

资料来源：http://www.askcaptainlim.com/-airplanes-aviation-39/945-why-the-flight-deck-of-an-airplane-is-called-a-qcockpitq.html

Unit Four

Aircraft Cabin

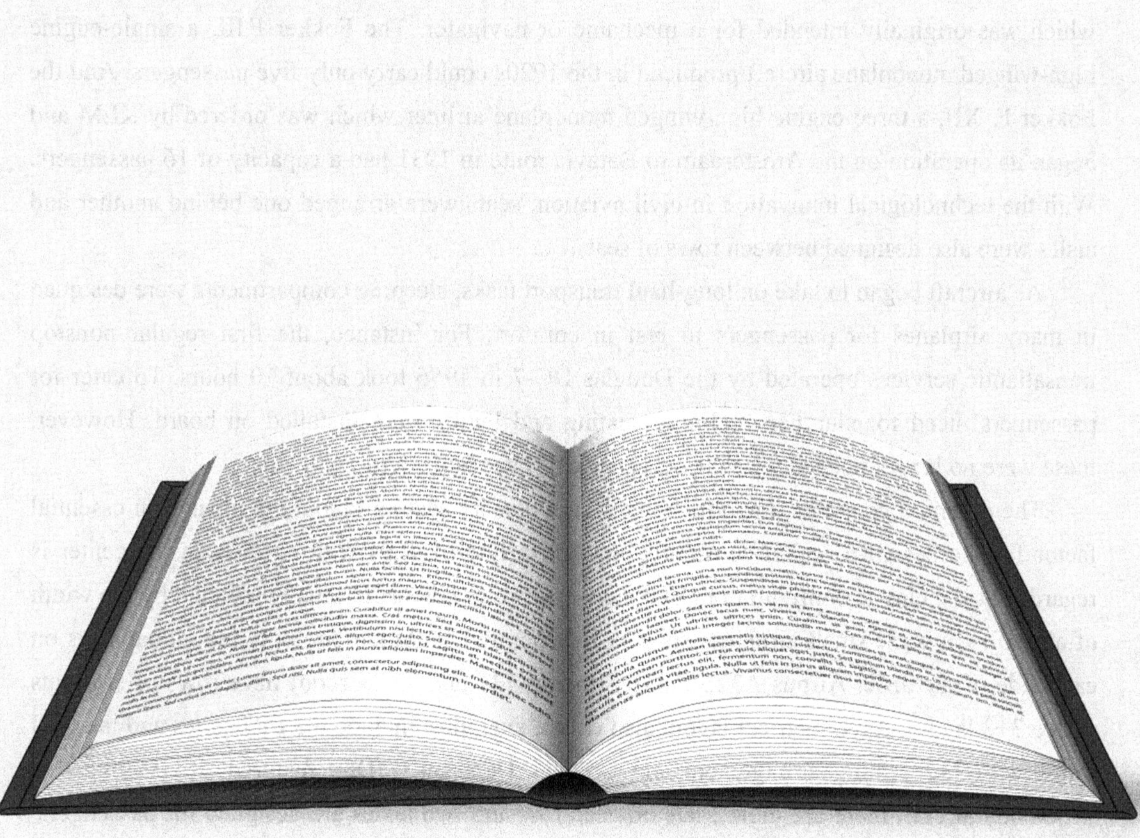

Text

Passage

A crucial factor that affects the revenue of an airline is the configuration of the aircraft cabin. The more passengers an airplane can carry, the more profits will be generated to the airline. Larger space devoted to the seating in the cabin also means higher price of the air tickets. Thus the airplane designer will take various factors into consideration. They will try to arrange the largest number of seating for passengers while maintaining their comfort and ensuring their safety.

In the early development stage of commercial passenger-carrying aviation, aircraft could carry only a small number of passengers. For instance, the Fokker F.II had an enclosed accommodation for four passengers, with a fifth seat alongside the pilot in his unenclosed cockpit which was originally intended for a mechanic or navigator. The Fokker F.III, a single-engine high-winged monoplane aircraft produced in the 1920s could carry only five passengers. And the Fokker F. XII, a three-engine high-winged monoplane airliner which was ordered by KLM and began its operation on the Amsterdam to Batavia route in 1931 had a capacity of 16 passengers. With the technological innovation in civil aviation, seats were arranged one behind another and aisles were also designed between rows of seats.

As aircraft began to take on long-haul transport tasks, sleeping compartments were designed in many airplanes for passengers to rest in comfort. For instance, the first regular nonstop transatlantic services operated by the Douglas DC-7 in 1956 took about 10 hours. To cater for passengers' need for slumber, reclining seating and bunks were installed on board. However, these were no longer needed with the emergence of later faster jets.

The potential economic benefits behind high-density seating layout are always an essential factor for the design of cabin configuration. And a line of seats with an aisle in the center is regarded as the classic configuration. The number of seats abreast is usually affected by the width of aircraft. On some small airplanes such as Beechcraft 1 900 there are only individual seats on each side of the aisle. Airbus A320 family, Boeing 727 and 737 aircraft have rows of six seats with a 3+3 layout. Asymmetrical layout also exists, examples include the ERJ series and the CRJ series with 1+2 seating arrangement and Douglas DC9 and MD80 featured 2+3 seating. On wide-body aircraft there are more seats on each row and two aisles are designed for passengers' passage. Very wide planes such as Boeing 747 or the Airbus A380 have rows of ten seats, typically in a 3+4+3 layout.

In many commercial flights, there are first-class, business class and economy class cabins for passengers with different needs. While some other airliners, such as commuter, shuttle aircraft, and charter flight, have only one class. The distinct travel class can be seen from the different seating layout.

New words

1. revenue ['revənju:]	n. 税收收入，财政收入，收益
2. enclosed [ɪn'kləʊzd]	v. 附上（enclose 的过去式和过去分词）
	adj. 被附上的；与世隔绝的
3. mechanic [mɪ'kænɪk]	n. 技工，机修工
	adj. 手工的
4. navigator ['nævɪgeɪtə]	n. 航海家；领航员；驾驶员
5. monoplane ['mɒnəpleɪn]	n.（航）单翼机
6. innovation [ɪnə'veɪʃn]	n. 创新，革新，改革；新方法
7. long-haul [lɔŋhɔl]	adj. 长途的，长距离的
8. slumber ['slʌmbə]	n. 睡眠，静止状态
	v. 睡眠，麻木
9. recline [rɪ'klaɪn]	v. 斜倚，斜躺
10. bunk [bʌŋk]	n. 铺位，床铺
	v. 睡在铺上，为……提供铺位
11. density ['densɪtɪ]	n. 密度
12. abreast [ə'brest]	adv. 肩并肩地
13. asymmetrical [eɪsɪ'metrɪkl]	adj. 不对称的，不匀称的
14. commuter [kə'mju:tə(r)]	n. 通勤者，经常乘公共车辆往返者
15. shuttle ['ʃʌt(ə)l]	n. 航天飞机
	v. 穿梭往返

Phrases and expressions

1. civil aviation	民用航空
2. sleeping compartment	卧室
3. seating layout	座位配置方案
4. classic configuration	经典的布局

Abbreviation

KLM Royal Dutch Airlines 荷兰皇家航空公司（KLM 为荷兰语首字母缩写）

Notes

1. For instance, the first regular nonstop transatlantic services operated by the Douglas DC-7 in 1956 took about 10 hours.

例如，1956 年道格拉斯 DC-7 首航横越大西洋直飞，全程大约需要 10 个小时。

2. The potential economic benefits behind high-density seating layout are always an essential factor for the design of cabin configuration.

高密度座椅配置所带来的潜在经济效益是客舱布局设计的一个重要考虑因素。

3. The distinct travel class can be seen from the different seating layout.

从不同的座位布局中即可看出明显的差别。

Exercises

I. Translate the following words or phrases into English.

1. 厨房
2. 紧急滑梯
3. 安全带
4. 急救箱
5. 灭火器
6. 餐桌
7. 扶手
8. 氧气面罩
9. 阅读灯
10. 呼叫按钮
11. 乘务人员
12. 旅客名单
13. 救生衣
14. 水上迫降
15. 水上逃生
16. 航站楼
17. 廊桥
18. 乘务长
19. 盥洗室
20. 遮阳板
21. 靠窗座位
22. 靠走道座位
23. 行李架
24. 紧急出口
25. 登机梯车

II. Read and translate the following short passages into Chinese.

1. In aviation, fatigue is a growing concern in flight operations. Beyond heavy workload and special environmental factors (high altitude, low air pressure, low oxygen partial pressure, noise, vibration etc.), cabin crews are exposed to irregular schedules, long working hours, jet lag and nigh work, conflicting with their body rhythms and contributes to sleep loss, fatigue and health and safety problems.

2. During a flight in an airliner, various external factors determine the way the passengers experience comfort, including specific environmental conditions such as temperature, noise, air quality and light to name but a few. Standards are then defined according to these factors to ensure that the conditions during a flight are not detrimental to the passengers' health. According to a recent study, coloured light could be used to intentionally create a sense of comfort among the passengers. The study states that coloured light could influence thermal sensations of people. It may convey the impression that the environmental temperature is warmer or cooler than it actually is while still providing thermal comfort.

3. Seats are frequently equipped with further amenities. Cabin seats may be equipped with a reclining mechanism to provide passenger comfort, either reclining mechanically (usually in economy class and short-haul first and business class) or electrically (usually in long-haul first class and business class). Most aircraft also feature trays for eating and reading, either in the seatback which folds down to form a small table in most economy class seats, or inside the armrest which folds out in most first class, business class, bulkhead, and exit row seats. On the back of each cabin seat, there is usually a pocket which may contain an in-flight magazine and safety instructions.

III. Answer the following questions based on the text.

1. What may affect the profits of an airline?
2. How many passengers can be carried in early aircraft?
3. What was designed for passengers to rest in DC-7 in 1956?
4. What is the seating layout on A320, CRJ, DC9 and B747?
5. How many types of cabin class do you know?

Supplementary Reading Material

The real reason why most plane seats are blue ——and other curious facts about plane cabins

Ever wonder why nearly all planes have blue seats? You've probably never noticed. Or why brand new models are still equipped with ash trays when it's illegal to smoke on board these days? Well wonder no more. Here we unpack some of lesser-known facts behind the design of an aircraft cabin.

Why seats are generally blue

From Ryanair and British Airways to American Airlines (the world's largest carrier), airlines across the board incorporate various shades of blue in their cabin seats, and it's no coincidence. There does appear to be some psychology behind it.

Blue is associated with the positive qualities of "trust, efficiency, serenity, coolness, reflection and calm," according to Colour Affects, the London-based consultancy run by Angela Wright, author of The Beginner's Guide to Colour Psychology.

Nigel Goode, lead aviation designer and co-founder at Priestman Goode, which has been delivering aircraft interiors for 30 years for airlines, including most recently the Airbus Airspace cabins, states: "Our job as designers is to reinforce the airline's brand and make it more recognisable, but our primary concern is to deliver an interior that maximises comfort to create a pleasant environment."

"It's all about making the travelling experience less stressful and blue is said to evoke a feeling of calm. While some of the more budget airlines might use brasher, bolder shades, most others go with muted tones. The overarching aim is to create a home-like relaxing feel, so airlines tend to use muted colours that feel domestic, natural and earthy for that reason."

It's also a trend that emerged decades ago and has simply stuck, he added: "Blue became the colour of choice because it's a conservative, non-contentious, corporate shade that symbolises being trustworthy and safe, so you see it used in all of the older airlines like British Airways."

The science behind the lighting

Cabin lighting is also geared towards creating a stress-free atmosphere on board, particularly in newer planes which have introduced soft LED lighting to replace the harsher light used in earlier models.

"There is definitely a science behind getting the right lighting on board, looking at the mix of colours used on board and how the light will reflect off the thread of the fabric," Mr. Goode explained.

Once all of the fabrics, textiles and finishes have been chosen, several colour workshops are held on aircraft interior mock-ups to trial the settings across a range of different lighting scenarios, from boarding and when pre-meal drinks and meals are served, to the sleeping hours.

"We work with lots of CMF (colour, materials and finish) specialists who look at various textiles and put a lot of work into choosing the best colour for the lighting. We want to make the seats restful but also somewhat interesting and not too bland to look at."

"Lighting and colour are particularly important in the built environment," noted British interior designer Jane Priestman, a former general manager and director of architecture and design for the British Airport Authority and British Rail.

"Our research in airports and railway stations has shown that the psychological power of colour and control of lighting can influence the mood of people," she said in a previous report.

Noise-cancelling walls

Several studies in recent years have exposed some of the detrimental effects of aircraft noise on health, including one back in 2010 which suggested that dying from a heart attack was more common among people with increased exposure to aircraft noise.

In recent years, new technology has revealed ways that aircraft noise could be reduced. Insulating the plane fuselage with a thin membrane, for example, can reduce the relentless hum of plane engines and make flying less noisy.

"We've also been looking at adding 'acoustic curtains'-padding across the plane to deaden the surrounding noises and the use of softer materials within the interior to help to deaden the sounds."

"And there's a lot of development around noise-cancelling features, both within the walls and in the individual seats near the headrests that may be used on planes in the future," Mr Goode said.

The importance of fabric

As a general rule, most long-haul carriers won't install leather seating because they can get unpleasantly sweaty. Synthetic fabrics breathe, which makes for a more comfortable experience.

Fabrics are chosen for their hard-wearing qualities and airlines tend to go with darker fabrics for maintenance reasons—it's much more of a bother to clear up a red wine spill on white fabric than on black, as most of us have discovered the hard way. Ergo, dark coloured seats mask dirt and therefore appear to be cleaner and longer-lasting than pale hues.

For the same reasons, patterned fabrics are favoured over plain ones for seat covers to mask wear and tear over the years.

"Lighter-coloured interiors, however, are more commonly found in first and business class seats, given not as many people fly in those cabins as they do in economy, where you'll see more of the darker shades," Mr. Goode explains.

All seats must pass the 16G test

Passenger seats with dummies strapped to them are put through the 16G test, a process which involves hurtling the seat down a 'sledge' ramp at high speeds to simulate a plane crash setting. All seats are required to withstand a 16g dynamic force.

The seats are sent down the slope at various angles to look at different crash scenarios and to see which parts of the seat need to be modified for maximum safety. All fabrics are also fire-tested to make sure they are quickly extinguishable, Mr. Goode explains.

What does the future hold for economy class

There are still areas in economy class which can be developed, given the limitations that many economy seat configurations currently come with, comfort being the big one.

"There's a big push at the moment for the magazine pouch to be relocated just a tiny bit higher to allow just a little bit more space," notes Mr. Goode.

There are also developments which involve moving those underseat metal boxes (which house all the wires for the in-flight entertainment) into walls or the flooring instead.

资料来源：https://www.telegraph.co.uk/travel/travel-truths/aircraft-cabin-design-why-seats-are-blue/

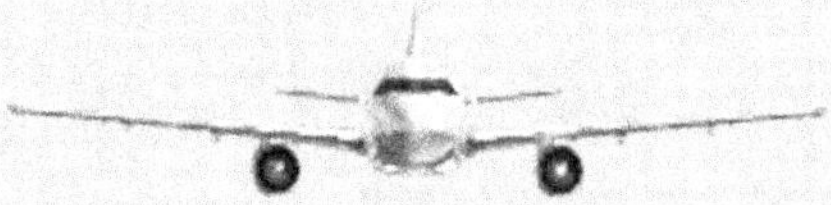

Unit Five
Cabin Service

Text

Passage

After decades of development, the cabin service has been quite different from the beginning. The first airlines imitated the palace-style luxury of the giant ocean liner before they can correctly define themselves. During the 1930s, passengers in elegant airships and delicate flying boats can enjoy leisurely meals by a full set of chef and stewards in magnificent dining rooms.

However, large-scale travel, aspiring after speed rather than comfort, need a large food and beverage supply. A large airline such as Singapore Airlines serves over 18 million inflight meals every year, investing about $500 million in cabin service.

Basically, inflight meals are prepared in vast catering centers which are usually rented at local airports at both ends of the air routes. In order to ensure the taste and texture of food, the food supply may be contracted by large hotels, restaurants or specialized companies. Meals must be loaded on the aircraft 20 to 40 minutes prior to departure, which are generally cold dishes and pre-cooked meals ready for reheating on board. Some meals such as pre-browned steaks need to be cooked in cabin ovens powered by the aircraft engines. In fact, not all airports are equipped with adequate food supply facilities, so frozen food has become the necessities on the flight. Frozen food needs to be heated for 30 seconds to thaw in the oven. In a sense, fresh food improves the standard of airline meal, but it can not be preserved for a long time. Once encountered flight delays, fresh food is likely to deteriorate. Some airlines replace fresh milk with milk powder, because in the pressurized cabin milk will soon become acid, and in some parts of the world milk can not be bought at any time.

Delicacy is an indispensable part of the flight, especially for the first-class and business-class travelers. More and more airlines are beginning to cooperate with Michelin chef and trying all out to design various menus. Singapore Airlines have ever invested $30 million in developing a new-style cabin kitchen.

The type of food varies depending upon the airline company and class of travel. Meals may be served on one tray or in multiple courses with no tray and with a tablecloth, metal cutlery, and glassware (generally in first and business classes). Often the food is reflective of the culture of the country the airline is based in. Tired of international popular grilled chicken and steak, travelers sometimes express strong interests in national dishes: most eastern airlines provide an alternative national menu.

The airline dinner typically includes meat (most commonly chicken or beef), fish, or pasta; a salad or vegetable; a small bread roll; and a dessert. Condiments (typically salt, pepper, and sugar) are supplied in small sachets or shakers. Caterers also produce alternative meals for passengers with restrictive diets. These must usually be ordered in advance, sometimes when buying the ticket. Some of the more common examples include:

- Cultural diets, such as Turkish, French, Italian, Chinese, Korean, Japanese or Indian style.
- Infant and baby meals. Some airlines also offer children's meals, containing foods that children will enjoy such as baked beans, mini-hamburgers and hot dogs.
- Medical diets, including low/high fiber, low fat/cholesterol, diabetic, peanut free, non-lactose, low salt/sodium, low-purine, low-calorie, low-protein, bland (non-spicy) and gluten-free meals.
- Religious diets, including kosher, halal, and Hindu, Buddhist and Jain vegetarian (sometimes termed Asian vegetarian) meals.
- Vegetarian and vegan meals. Some airlines do not offer a specific meal for non-vegan vegetarians; instead, they are given a vegan meal.

Food on board is usually free on full-service Asian airlines and on almost all long-distance flights, while they might cost extra on low-cost airlines or European full-service airline flights. Quality may also fluctuate due to shifts in the economics of the airline industry. Air China has reported that each domestic flight's meal requires RMB50 (US$7.30) while international flights require RMB70 (US$10). However, this figure varies from airline to airline, as some have reported costs to be as low as US$3.50.

The flight crew may be served a more varied food menu. To avoid food poisoning at the same time, the captain and the co-pilot usually eat different meals and are banned to eat shellfish.

Following an international standard time, mealtimes depend on departure time. In event of turbulence, they may be adjusted. Heating and supply time are reasonable timed so as not to provide tepid food to passengers.

Everyday the first service vehicles to reach the aircraft apron are usually the catering trucks. The staff moved the used utensils and rubbish and put the new replacement on the plane. That's really a large project. British Airways is said to deal with about 500,000 flatware, 168,000 glasses, 50,000 dishes, 40,000 cups and saucers, and cleaning about 100 tons of linen and blankets every week.

New words

1. airship ['eəʃɪp]　　n. 飞艇，飞船
2. catering ['keɪtərɪŋ]　　n. 提供饮食及服务
3. deteriorate [dɪ'tɪəriəreɪt]　　vi. 恶化，变坏

4. delicacy ['delɪkəsi] n. 美味佳肴
5. indispensable [ˌɪndɪ'spensəbl] adj. 不可缺少的；绝对必要的
6. chef [ʃef] n. 厨师，大师傅
7. cutlery ['kʌtləri] n. 刀具，刀叉
8. pasta ['pæstə] n. 意大利面食
9. condiment ['kɒndɪm(ə)nt] n. 调味品，佐料
10. sachet ['sæʃeɪ] n.（塑料或纸质）密封小袋
11. Turkish ['tɜ:kɪʃ] adj. 土耳其的，土耳其人的，土耳其语的
12. infant ['ɪnfənt] adj. 婴儿的，幼儿的
13. fiber ['faɪbə] n. 纤维，纤维物质
14. cholesterol [kə'lestərɒl] n. 胆固醇
15. diabetic [ˌdaɪə'betɪk] adj. 糖尿病的
n. 糖尿病患者
16. lactose ['læktəʊs] n. 乳糖
17. sodium ['səʊdiəm] n. 钠
18. purine ['pjʊrɪn] n. 嘌呤，咖啡碱
19. calorie ['kæləri] n. 卡路里；大卡；卡（热量单位）
20. protein ['prəʊti:n] n. 蛋白质
21. bland [blænd] adj. 清淡的，温和的
22. gluten ['glu:t(ə)n] n. 面筋；麸质；谷蛋白
23. kosher ['kəʊʃə] adj. 犹太教所规定允许的
24. halal ['hælæl] n. 伊斯兰教律法的合法食物
25. Hindu ['hɪndu:] adj. 印度教的；印度人的
26. Buddhist ['bʊdɪst] adj. 佛教的；佛教徒的；佛法的
27. Jain [dʒain] adj. 耆那教的，耆那教徒的
28. vegetarian [ˌvedʒi'teəriən] adj. 素食者的；素菜的
29. vegan ['vi:g(ə)n] n. 严格的素食主义者
30. fluctuate ['flʌktʃueɪt] vi. 波动；涨落
31. shellfish ['ʃelfɪʃ] n. 贝类动物；甲壳类动物；甲壳类（食物）
32. tepid ['tepɪd] adj. 微温的；不冷不热的
33. utensil [ju: 'tensl] n. 器皿；器具，用具；家庭厨房用具
34. flatware ['flætweə] n. 扁平的餐具（尤指刀、叉、匙等）

Phrases and expressions

1. ocean liner 远洋定期客轮；邮船
2. air route 航线
3. cold dish 凉菜；冷盘；小吃

4. national dish 国家代表菜
5. low-cost airlines 廉价航空；低成本航空公司；低费用航空公司
6. domestic flight 国内航班
7. catering truck 航空食品车

Abbreviations

SA Singapore Airlines 新加坡航空公司
AC Air China 中国国际航空公司
BA British Airways 英国航空公司

Notes

1. During the 1930s, passengers in elegant airships and delicate flying boats can enjoy leisurely meals by a full set of chef and stewards in magnificent dining rooms.

在 20 世纪 30 年代，在优雅的飞艇和精致的飞行船上，乘客可以在华丽的餐厅里悠闲用餐，享受厨师和服务员提供的美食。

2. A large airline such as Singapore Airlines serves over 18 million inflight meals every year, investing about US$500 million in cabin service.

大航空公司如新加坡航空公司，每年要提供超过 1 800 万份的航空餐食，投资大约 5 亿美元在客舱服务上。

3. More and more airlines are beginning to cooperate with Michelin chef and trying all out to design various menus.

越来越多的航空公司开始与米其林厨师合作，并努力设计各种菜单。

4. British Airways is said to deal with about 500,000 flatware, 168,000 glasses, 50,000 dishes, 40,000 cups and saucers, and cleaning about 100 tons of linen and blankets every week.

据说英国航空公司每周要处理大约 50 万套餐具、16.8 万只玻璃杯、5 万张盘子、4 万套杯碟，清理大约 100 吨亚麻餐布和毛毯。

Exercises

I. Write down the full name of each abbreviation and translate it into Chinese.

1. BBML
2. CHML
3. MOML
4. HNML
5. KSML
6. VML
7. DBML

8. FFML
9. red meat
10. soft drink
11. alcohol drink
12. main dish
13. mineral water
14. purified water

II. Analyze the following passages grammatically.

1. However, large-scale travel, aspiring after speed rather than comfort, need a large food and beverage supply.

2. Meals may be served on one tray or in multiple courses with no tray and with a tablecloth, metal cutlery, and glassware (generally in first and business classes).

III. Answer the following questions based on the text.

1. Who are responsible for making the cabin meals?
2. When should the cabin meals be loaded on the aircraft?
3. When should the passengers with restrictive diets order their special meals?
4. What dose religious diet include?
5. Why do the captain and the co-pilot usually eat different meals?

Supplementary Reading Material

What does a Flight Attendant do?

What is a Flight Attendant?

A flight attendant is someone whose primary duty is to ensure the safety and comfort of passengers during an airline flight. They are part of the cabin crew for the plane, a team of personnel who operate a commercial, business, or even military aircraft while traveling domestically or internationally. Since the career began in 1912, male flight attendants have also been known as stewards or air hosts and females as stewardesses or air hostesses. Flight attendants are specially trained for the aircraft in which they work, since passenger safety is their foremost concern.

What does a Flight Attendant do?

Almost all of the flight attendant's duties are safety-related, though customer service is also important. Approximately one hour before each flight, attendants are briefed by their captain. Weather conditions, possible turbulence, flight duration, and other factors that may affect the upcoming flight are discussed in detail. They are also briefed on safety details and emergency equipment supplies relevant to the aircraft they will be flying. A list of passengers is verified and attendants are notified if any special needs passengers, small children, or VIPs will be boarding the flight.

After the briefing, flight attendants inspect the aircraft, ensuring the safety equipment is in place and working properly. If a piece of equipment, such as a fire extinguisher, is found unserviceable, flight attendants must replace the item prior to takeoff. Once passengers are called to board, flight attendants assist with the boarding process. They aid any special needs passengers, children, or VIPs to ensure they receive the proper care while boarding. Tickets and seating positions are verified, and attendants check for both accuracy and possible fraudulent or stolen tickets. Attendants also monitor passengers; they are trained to detect suspicious behaviour and evidence of malicious intent, to prevent hijacking or terrorism. In addition, they help passengers load carry-on baggages, checking that each adheres to aircraft or airline size and weight restrictions.

Flight attendants are also responsible for briefing the passengers on safety standards specific to the aircraft in a safety demonstration. Passengers are made aware of how to locate their nearest emergency exit, how to properly buckle their safety belts, what to do in the event of turbulence, how to operate safety vests or flotation devices, and how to use the drop-down oxygen masks. In some cases, passengers will watch a short video covering this information while the flight attendant monitors their behaviour. After the safety demonstration, attendants secure the cabin, making sure electronic devices and cell phones are turned off, carry-ons are stowed correctly, seats are in an upright position, and tray tables are stowed. The entire procedure, from boarding to takeoff, is known as pre take off service.

After the plane is safely in the air, flight attendants check for passenger comfort. They deliver headphones or pillows to passengers who request them and serve food or drinks. In addition to serving the customers, flight attendants must conduct regular safety checks and listen for unusual noises. Once the plane begins its descent, attendants must ensure all trash has been removed from the cabin and seats are in their correct positions before performing a final safety check. After landing, attendants assist passengers in safely deplaning the aircraft.

What is the workplace of a Flight Attendant like?

Since airlines operate day and night and year-round, flight attendants must have a flexible schedule. Generally, they work no more than 12 hours per day, but in some cases, especially in the event of oversea international flights, they may work 14 hours or more. Attendants also work on holidays and weekends and typically fly for 65 to 90 hours per month, with another 50 hours spent on the ground preparing or waiting for flights.

资料来源：https://www.sokanu.com/careers/flight-attendant/

Unit Six

Aerial Navigation (I)

Text

Passage

To be able to find his way around the skies, a pilot needs to know his position and his direction. Finding direction is easy using the simple magnetic compass, and there is at least one of these on every flight deck. Another kind of aircraft compass uses a gyroscope. Modern aircraft compasses are complex and highly efficient. Finding position is more difficult for a pilot than finding direction, and needs complex aids.

Air travel was always limited as long as pilots had to navigate using only compass bearings, maps and visual pointers. Planes equipped with radio have the aviator's equivalent of the mariner's light-house to find position, with one advantage: radio waves do not need to be visible to be effective. They can travel all over the world either in long waves—used in long-range navigation that curve around the earth's surface, or in short waves which tend to travel in straight lines and are used in short-range navigation systems.

But even the most sophisticated radio navigation system has something in common with the simple method of leaning out of the cockpit to take a visual bearing on a church or river: both depend upon ground based aids. Ultra-modern devices such as Doppler radar and weather radar are entirely self-contained, and so are the inertial guidance systems whose accurate measuring devices can record barely perceptible accelerations in aircraft speed.

In future years these systems will be completed by a network of very low frequency Omega radio stations, by laser devices and by satellite systems.

Dead-reckoning (sometimes called "ded"—for deductive—reckoning). The oldest and simplest form of aerial navigation is still used by pilots of light aircraft. It depends on recognizable ground landmarks. The pilot plots his track on the map before take off, and uses his compass, to file in the right direction. Knowing his speed will enable him to calculate when he should fly over certain landmarks, and so check his progress.

The wind, carrying the aircraft off course, or causing sudden speed-ups or slow-downs, upsets such simple navigation. By relating his last known position to the direction he has flown, and his speed, the pilot will determine an approximate position several times during the flight. This becomes the centre of a circle, called a circle of uncertainty, whose radius is about ten percent of the distance flown since the last landmark.

New words

1. aerial ['ɛəriəl]	adj. 航空的，空中的
2. navigation [nævi'geiʃ(ə)n]	n. 领航，导航，航行
3. gyroscope ['dʒairəskəup]	n. 陀螺（仪）
4. bearing ['bɛriŋ]	n. 方位（角）
5. visual ['viʒjuəl]	adj. 目视的，可见的
6. pointer ['pɔintə]	n. 指针，指示器
7. mariner ['mærinə]	n. 海员，水手
8. lighthouse ['laithaus]	n. 灯塔
9. advantage [əd'va:ntidʒ]	n. 有利条件，好处，优势
10. ultra ['ʌltrə]	adj. 极端的，过分的
11. radar ['reida:]	n. 雷达；无线电探测器
12. inertial [i'n ɜ:ʃ(ə)l]	adj. 惯性的；不活泼的
13. perceptible [pə'sɛptəbl]	adj. 可感觉的；可理解的；看得见的
14. laser ['leizə]	n. 激光（器）
15. reckoning ['rek(ə)niŋ]	n. 计算，航迹推算
16. deductive [di'dʌktiv]	adj. 推测的，推论的，演绎的
17. landmark ['læn(d)ma:k]	n. 地标，界标，陆标
18. upset [ʌp'set]	v. 使烦恼，使扰乱
19. uncertainty [ʌn'sə:tnti]	n. 不定性，不可靠性，不精确，误差
20. radius ['reidɪəs]	n. 半径，有效航程

Phrases and expressions

1. aerial navigation	空中领航，空中航行
2. to find direction (position)	定向（位）
3. magnetic compass	磁罗盘
4. compass (visual) bearing	罗盘（目视）方位
5. radio navigation system	无线电导航系统
6. in common with	与……有共同之处；与……相同
7. ground based aids	地面设备
8. ultra-modern device	超现代化装置
9. Doppler radar	多普勒雷达
10. weather radar	气象雷达
11. inertial guidance systems	惯性制导系统
12. very low frequency	特低频，超长波
13. radio station	无线电台

14. laser devices　　激光装置
15. satellite systems　　卫星系统
16. dead-reckoning　　推测领航
17. light aircraft　　轻型飞机，小型飞机
18. ground landmark　　地面标志
19. off course　　偏离航线

Notes

1. Air travel was always limited as long as pilots had to navigate using only compass bearing, maps and visual pointers.

如果驾驶员只会用罗盘、地图和目视指示器进行导航，空中旅行就总是会受到限制。

2. But even the most sophisticated radio navigation system has something in common with the simple method of leaning out of the cockpit to take a visual bearing on a church or river.

但是即便是最复杂的无线电导航系统也和将头探出驾驶舱去测定某个教堂或河流的目视方位这种简单的方法有共同之处。

3. Knowing his speed will enable him to calculate when he should fly over certain landmarks, and so check his progress.

驾驶员知道了飞行的速度就能计算何时该飞越某个地标，并以此来校正他的进程。

Exercises

I. Read and explain the following passages.

1. Laser navigation

Laser "gyros" may soon provide a navigation system with no moving parts; three mounted in an aircraft, can detect the slightest movement. They consist of triangular tubes with mirrors at each angle. Two laser beams, transmitted in opposite directions, take the same to travel round the triangle, but when rotated by aircraft movement one beam takes longer to complete a circuit.

2. Satellite navigation system

Navstar, several of its satellites already in orbit, is one of various satellite systems under development. It may be fully operational by the 1990s. Its final 24 satellites, orbiting simultaneously 10,000 miles high, will provide continuous high quality position fixes. When perfected the system will enable a pilot to know where he is with-in 20 ft, the width of a Boeing 747.

II. Translate the following terms into Chinese.

1. Navigation is the science of finding one's way from one place to another by means of landmarks and instruments.

2. The basic direction-finding device in terrestrial navigation is the compass of which there

are two types: the magnetic and gyro compasses.

3. Orbiting satellites, equipped with navigational transmitters, at present being perfected can provide position fixing with an accuracy down to 20 feet.

4. Home (or Homing): Flight toward a NAVAID, without correcting for wind, by adjusting the aircraft heading so that it maintains the same relative bearing.

III. Analyze the following passages grammatically.

1. Finding position is more difficult for a pilot than finding direction, and needs complex aids.

2. Plans equipped with radio have the aviator's equivalent of the mariner's light-house to find position.

3. They can travel all over the world either in long waves—used in long-range navigation—that curve around the earth's surface, or in short waves which tend to travel in straight lines and are used in short-range navigation systems.

4. Ultra-modern devices such as Doppler radar and weather radar are entirely self-contained, and so are the inertial guidance systems whose accurate measuring devices can record barely perceptible accelerations in aircraft speed.

5. By relating his last known position to the direction he has flown, and his speed, the pilot will determine an approximate position several times during the flight.

Supplementary Reading Material

Airmanship in Night Flying

The idea of airmanship as differentiated from Human Factors is a concept of operational and physical situational awareness. Airmanship refers to the consideration given to factors not covered explicitly in rules or by the physiological or socio-technological subjects covered in normal discussions about human factors. For night flying this would include acknowledgement of the additional restrictions placed on equipment, flight planning and emergency actions.

For example in a PPL night flight in a basic light aircraft the legal requirements require minimum equipment as listed above in the rules but airmanship would add other items. These may include carrying life jackets in case a diversion or emergency requires flight near or over water and the wearing life jackets rather than just carrying them in the aircraft. At night an emergency landing may be safer in the water which is relatively flat and obstacle free rather than on land. Statistics show water landings are often more survivable than many expect and it is often the lack of floatation after the event that results in fatalities rather than the landing or impact itself.

Another consideration would be carrying fuel that included the diversion in the onboard total before the legal minimums e.g. flight detail + diversion + reserve + unusable.

Good airmanship would also dictate the use of a flight plan or similar for effective flight following. Whereas a flight by day from a supervised airfield or training centre may be easily monitored the fact that less flying occurs at night may mean less supervision and awareness. A flight plan would allow Search and Rescue monitoring by Flight Information or Air Traffic Control.

Additionally, planning for the flight might also need to consider airspace boundary and usage changes brought about by the change in status of airspace after sunset, whether control towers are active or not, whether alternates are equipped with lighting and services and the pilot may also wish to prepare a chart with diversion routes and safe altitudes already marked out.

None of the examples included above include factoring required by law or general human factors topics, yet should be part of the basic considerations undertaken by a pilot prior to flying privately at night.

Many of these considerations may be covered for commercial flights by operational requirements, reflecting the higher planning standards required and the increased level of flight supervision applied to such flights.

资料来源：http://aviationknowledge.wikidot.com/aviation:night-flying-part-2-airmanship

Unit Seven

Aerial Navigation (II)

Text

Passage

Radio navigation is widely utilized in commercial flights. By tuning the radio navigation equipment on board, the pilots could receive a signal from a ground-stationed NAVAID, through which the pilots could not only realize whether the course is to or from the station, but also understand whether the aircraft deviates from the course. Then the pilots could make adjustment to correct the direction.

One of the most common navigation systems is called VOR, which provides magnetic bearing information to and from the station. When DME is also installed with a VOR, the NAVAID is referred to as a VOR/ DME. When military tactical air navigation (TACAN) equipment is installed with a VOR, the NAVAID is known as a VORTAC. And DME is always an integral part of a VORTAC. Before the advent of these systems, the radio compass low-frequency radio receiver combined with the NDB was the main system used for aerial navigation.

The signals sent by the low-frequency radio receiver direct the pilot to home from the station. Then the pilot could navigate off the station by following a series of procedures. However, these non-directional radio beacons are sensitive to atmospheric and other types of interferences such as poor signals or the disturbance from other stations, which may cause the malfunction of the instruments on board.

INS, LORAN and Decca are three of the common transoceanic navigation systems used in civil aviation.

INS is a self-contained navigation system which requires no external references to determine its position, orientation, or velocity after initialization. Thus it is immune to jamming and deception and suitable for long-range flight over water or land areas without adequate radio station on the ground.

The LORAN system is a hyperbolic radio navigation system developed in the US during World War II, which provides an improved range with finer accuracy compared with the older systems. The great distances and lack of useful navigation points in the Pacific Ocean led to a widespread use of LORAN for both marine and air navigation during the Pacific War. Later an improved version LORAN-C with better performance (the original retroactively became LORAN-A) became popular and began to replace the old one.

Like LORAN, the Decca navigation system is also a hyperbolic radio navigation system which allows ships and aircraft to determine their position by receiving radio signals from fixed navigational beacons but offers better accuracy than the competing LORAN system. The system was developed in the UK and first deployed by the Royal Navy during World War II. Aircraft using LORAN or Decca is equipped with facilities to receive special signals from transmitting stations indicating the exact position of the plane.

Since the 1960s, navigation has increasingly moved to satellite navigation systems. One of the global navigation satellite systems is GPS, a space-based radio navigation system with better accuracy than any previous land-based system and available at almost all locations on the earth. It requires only a few dozen satellites to provide worldwide coverage. Its distinct advantages have aroused worldwide attention and this type of navigation system enjoys a very promising prospect.

New words

1. utilize ['jutəlaɪz]	v. 利用
2. tune [tjuːn]	v. 调整
3. course [kɔːs]	n. 航线，航路
4. deviate ['diːvɪeɪt]	v. 背离，偏离
5. integral ['ɪntɪgrəl]	adj. 必需的，不可或缺的；完整的
6. advent ['ædvənt]	n. 出现，到来
7. atmospheric [ætməs'ferɪk]	adj. 大气的，大气层的
8. interference [ɪntə'fɪər(ə)ns]	n. 干扰，冲突，干涉
9. malfunction [mæl'fʌŋ(k)ʃ(ə)n]	n. 故障，失灵
10. orientation [ˌɔːrɪən'teɪʃ(ə)n]	n. 方向，定向；情况介绍
11. velocity [və'lɒsəti]	n. 速度
12. initialization [ɪˌnɪʃəlaɪ'zeɪʃən]	n. 初始化
13. deception [dɪ'sepʃ(ə)n]	n. 欺骗，诱惑，伪装
14. hyperbolic [ˌhaɪpə'bɒlɪk]	adj. 双曲线的；夸张的
15. marine [mə'riːn]	adj. 海产的，海运的，航海的
16. deploy [dɪ'plɒɪ]	v. 部署，调动
17. satellite ['sætəlaɪt]	n. 卫星
18. prospect ['prɒspekt]	n. 前途，预期；景色

Phrases and expressions

1. radio navigation	无线电导航
2. magnetic bearing	磁向位
3. radio compass	无线电罗盘

4. poor signal　　信号太差
5. be immune to　　不受……影响
6. Royal Navy　　皇家海军

Abbreviations

1. NAVAID　Navigational Aid　导航设备
2. VOR　Very-high-frequency Omnidirectional Range　甚高频全向信标
3. DME　Distance Measuring Equipment　测距仪
4. TACAN　Tactical Air Navigation　塔康（战术空中导航）
5. INS　Inertial Navigation System　惯性导航系统
6. LORAN　Long Range Navigation　罗兰（远程导航系统）
7. GPS　Global Position System　全球定位系统
8. Decca　Decca Navigation System　台卡（低频联系波相位双曲线定位系统）

Notes

1. By tuning the radio navigation equipment on board, the pilot could receive a signal from a ground-stationed NAVAID, through which the pilots could not only realize whether the course is to or from the station, but also he could understand whether the aircraft deviates from the course.

飞行员通过调节机载无线电导航设备接收地面导航台发射的信号。依据这个信号，飞行员不仅能够知道飞机是向台还是背台，也能够了解飞机是否偏离航线。

2. INS is a self-contained navigation system which requires no external references to determine its position, orientation, or velocity after initialization.

惯性导航系统（INS）是一种自主导航系统，一旦启动该系统不依赖于外界就可以确定自身位置、方向或速度。

3. The LORAN system is a hyperbolic radio navigation system developed in the US during World War II, which provides an improved range with finer accuracy compared with the older systems.

远距离无线电导航系统（LORAN）是一种双曲线无线电导航系统，由美国在二战期间研发。与旧系统相比，该系统提供更远的航程，精确性也更高。

Exercises

I. Write down the full name of each abbreviation and translate it into Chinese.

1. ILS
2. IGS
3. VOR
4. NDB

5. DME
6. PAR
7. ASR
8. GPS
9. GNSS
10. RNAV
11. RNP
12. LDA

II. Try to learn the following position report.

1. Position OBLIK at 0646, maintaining FL310, estimating ZF 0658, WUH next.
2. Position 42N165E at 0800, FL390, estimating 44N 180E at 0900 45N 170W next.

III. Read and translate the following short passages into Chinese.

1. The modern commercial airplane cockpit is a technological marvel. Computer screens and keypads have replaced many of the old switches, dials and instruments. Yet most commercial airline pilots still arrive at work carrying 70-year-old technology: printed flight charts held in leather binders. The division of Boeing Co. is developing a new three-dimensional "synthetic vision" system that will replace the traditional flight chart, both in its print and electronic forms. The system will be a large computer monitor that displays a realistic image of the terrain around the aircraft and provides other navigational information. At first, it's likely to show up in the cockpits of corporate aircraft, eventually making its way into commercial airliners.

2. Aircrafts are usually controlled by basic control surfaces like ailerons, elevators and rudders, supported by additional control surfaces: stabilizer, spoiler, flaps and by control of the engine thrust. Aircraft motion for various degrees of freedom is controlled by single or multiple control surfaces. However, navigation, communication, radar and other special equipment are severely limited if the pilot has to work continually on the physical manipulation of the controls. Automatic flight control and stabilization systems ease the pilot's workload and provide aircraft stability at all speeds. Automatic Flight Control Systems are capable of flying the aircraft by radio navigation aids, correcting for wind, and making pilot unaided landings.

IV. Answer the following questions based on the text.

1. What does NAVAID stand for? Why is it important for flight?
2. What are the disadvantages of non-directional radio beacons?
3. What navigation systems can be used when aircraft fly across ocean?
4. How do you understand INS?
5. What is GPS?

Supplementary Reading Material

Radio Navigation

With aircraft equipped with radio navigation aids (NAVAIDS), pilots can navigate more accurately than with dead reckoning alone. Radio NAVAIDS come in handy in low visibility conditions and act as a suitable backup method for general aviation pilots that prefer dead reckoning. They are also more precise. There are different types of radio NAVAIDS used in aviation:

ADF/NDB: The most elementary form of radio navigation is the ADF/NDB pair. The ADF instrument is basically an arrow pointer placed over a compass card-type display. The ADF/NDB is an outdated NAVAID, and it's a system prone to errors. Since its range is line-of-sight, a pilot can get erroneous readings while flying in mountainous terrain or too far from the station.

VOR: Next to GPS, the VOR system is probably the most commonly used NAVAIDS in the world. VOR, short for VHF Omnidirectional Range, is a radio-based NAVAID that operates in the very-high-frequency range. VORs are more accurate than NDBs and less prone to errors, although the reception is still susceptible to line-of-sight only.

DME: Distance Measuring Equipment is one of the most simple and valuable NAVAIDS to date. A single DME station can handle up to 100 aircraft at one time, and they usually co-exist with VOR ground stations.

ILS: An instrument landing system (ILS) is an instrument approach system used to guide aircraft down to the runway from the approach phase of flight. ILS systems are widely in use today as one of the most accurate approach systems available.

GPS: The global positioning system has become the most valuable method of navigation in the modern aviation world. GPS has proven to be tremendously reliable and precise and is probably the most common NAVAID in use today.

The global positioning system uses 24 US Department of Defense satellites to provide precise location data, such as aircraft position, track, speed, and to pilots. GPS has become a preferred method of navigating due to the accuracy and ease of use. Though there are errors associated with GPS, they are rare. GPS systems can be used anywhere in the world, even in mountainous terrain, and they aren't prone to the errors of radio NAVAIDS, such as line-of-sight and electrical interference.

Practical Use of NAVAIDS: Pilots will fly under visual flight rules (VFR) or instrument flight rules (IFR), depending on the weather conditions. During visual meteorological conditions (VMC), a pilot might fly by using pilotage and dead reckoning alone, or he might use radio navigation or GPS navigation techniques. Basic navigation is taught in the early stages of flight training.

In instrument meteorological conditions (IMC) or while flying IFR, a pilot will need to rely on cockpit instruments, such as a VOR or GPS system. Because flying in the clouds and navigating with these instruments can be tricky, a pilot must earn an FAA Instrument Rating to fly in IMC conditions legally.

Currently, the FAA is emphasizing new training for general aviation pilots in technologically advanced aircraft (TAA). TAA is an aircraft that have advanced high-tech systems on board, such as GPS. Even light sport aircrafts are coming out of the factory with advanced equipments these days. It can be confusing and dangerous for a pilot to attempt to use these modern cockpit systems in-flight without additional training, and current FAA training standards haven't kept up with this issue.

The FAA's updated FITS program finally addressed the issue, although the program is still voluntary.

资料来源：https://www.thebalancecareers.com/how-do-pilots-navigate-282803

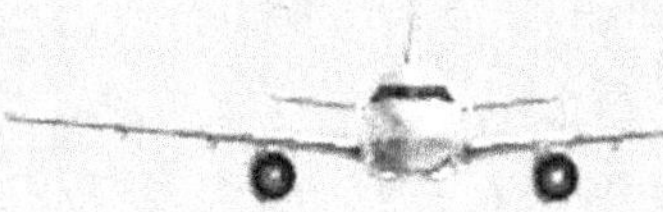

Unit Eight

Air Traffic Control

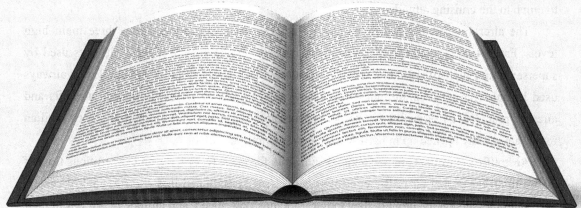

Text

Passage

In the vast expanse of the sky, the aircrafts seem to freely fly to anywhere they wish to fly, however, this is not the case. Aircrafts are like vehicles running on the ground, which must obey the traffic rules and accept the police's commands, they must also obey the air traffic rules and be commanded and dispatched by professionals. Air traffic controllers are the professionals, who are essential to keep aircrafts separated in the sky around the airport where is full of aircrafts flying at different speeds in different directions and crossing over each other at different heights.

Air traffic control is a service provided by ground-based air traffic controllers who direct aircraft on the ground and through controlled airspace, and provide advisory services to aircraft in non-controlled airspace. In many countries, ATC provides services to all private, military, and commercial aircrafts operating within its airspace. Depending on the type of flight and the class of airspace, ATC may issue instructions that pilots are required to obey, or advisories (known as flight information in some countries) that pilots may, at their discretion, disregard.

The interval between two take-off aircrafts is strictly regulated. The same type of aircrafts, which usually take off in two different directions, has a minimum time interval of one minute. If they take off in the same direction, however, the time interval is two minutes. Producing tail airflow disturbance, a wide-body jet departure usually holds back a light aircraft departure by 10 minutes. When the aircraft is safely separated and climbing in accordance with the standard instrument departure, it will be handed over to the first radar sector controller for his permission to climb to the cruising altitude.

The aircraft generally follow certain air routes, which are divided into three main high levels. From 45,000 to 75,000 feet (available airspace limit) are the highest altitudes used by supersonic and high-flying commercial jets; below the highest altitudes are the lower airways used by subsonic jets; the altitudes below are usually used by slower turboprop aircrafts and aircrafts propelled by propeller. As many airspaces are used strictly for military purposes, civilian routes are usually opened up in narrow gaps between military areas.

Air traffic controllers are personnel responsible for the safe, orderly, and expeditious flow of air traffic in the global air traffic control system. Usually stationed in air traffic control centers and control towers on the ground, they monitor the position, speed, and altitude of aircraft in their assigned airspace visually and by radar, and give directions to the pilots by radio.

In most nations air traffic controllers who are stationed in air traffic control center are known as "area," "en route," or, colloquially in the US, "center" controllers. Area controllers are responsible for the safety of aircraft at higher altitudes, in the en route phase of their flight surrounding busier airports and airspaces. Area controllers may also handle aircraft at lower altitudes as well as air traffic around small airports that do not have their own towers or approach controllers.

Aerodrome or Tower controllers control aircraft within the immediate vicinity of the airport and use visual observation from the airport tower. The tower's airspace is often a 5-nautical-mile (9.3 km) radius around the airport, but can vary greatly in size and shape depending on traffic configuration and volume. The tower positions are typically split into many different positions such as Flight Data/Clearance Delivery, Ground Control, and Local Control (known as Tower by the pilots); at busier facilities, a limited radar approach control position may be needed.

The position of air traffic controller is one that requires highly specialized knowledge, skills, and abilities. Controllers apply separation rules to keep aircraft at a safe distance from each other in their area of responsibility and move all aircrafts safely and efficiently through their assigned sectors of airspace, as well as on the ground. Because controllers have an incredibly large responsibility while on duty (often in aviation, "on position") and make countless real-time decisions on a daily basis, the ATC profession is consistently regarded around the world as one of the most mentally challenging careers, and can be notoriously stressful depending on many variables (equipment, configurations, weather, traffic volume, human factors, etc.). Many controllers, however, would cite high salaries, and a very large, unique, and privileged degree of autonomy as major advantages of their jobs.

Communication is a vital part of the job: controllers are trained to focus on the exact words that pilots and other controllers speak, because a single misunderstanding about altitude levels or runway numbers can have tragic consequences. Controllers communicate with the pilots of aircraft using a push-to-talk radio telephony system which has many attendant issues, such as the fact that only one transmission can be made on a frequency at a time and can either merge or block each other and become unintelligible.

Although local languages are used in ATC communications, the default language of aviation worldwide is English. Controllers who do not speak English as a first language are generally expected to show a certain minimum level of competency with the language.

Teamwork plays a major role in a controller's job, not only with other controllers and air traffic staff, but with pilots, engineers and managers.

New words

1. dispatch [dɪ'spætʃ] vt. 派遣，调度
2. airspace ['eəspeɪs] n. 领空，（某国的）空域

3. disregard [dɪsrɪ'gɑ:d] vt. 不顾；不理会；漠视，忽视
4. interval ['ɪntəv(ə)l] n. 间隔；幕间休息
5. airflow ['eəfləʊ] n. 空气流动，（尤指行驶中车辆外的）气流
6. turboprop ['tɜ:bəʊprɒp] n. 涡轮螺旋桨发动机；涡轮机螺旋桨式飞机
7. expeditious [ˌɛkspə'dɪʃəs] adj. 迅速而有效率的，迅速完成的
8. colloquially [kə'ləʊkwɪəlɪ] adv. 用白话，用通俗语
9. aerodrome ['eərədrəʊm] n. （小）飞机场；航空站
10. radius ['reɪdiəs] n. 半径范围
11. configuration [kənˌfɪgə'reɪʃ(ə)n] n. 配置；布局，构造
12. notoriously [nəʊ'tɔ:rɪəslɪ] adv. 众所周知地
13. privileged ['prɪvəlɪdʒd] adj. 享有特权的；特许的，专用的
14. push-to-talk n. 即按即说；按压通话
15. radiotelephony ['reɪdɪəʊtɪ'lefɒnɪ] n. 无线电话
16. default [dɪ'fɔ:lt] n. 默认

Phrases and expressions

1. air traffic controller 空中交通管制员
2. tail airflow 尾流
3. wide-body jet 宽体客机
4. nautical mile 海里

Abbreviations

1. ATC air traffic control 空中交通管制
2. SID standard instrument departure 标准仪表离场

Notes

1. Producing tail airflow disturbance, a wide-body jet departure usually holds back a light aircraft departure by 10 minutes.

由于宽体客机起飞时会产生尾部气流，后面起飞的轻型飞机通常要晚起飞 10 分钟来避开气流。

2. From 45,000 to 75,000 feet (available airspace limit) are the highest altitudes used by supersonic and high-flying commercial jets.

从 45 000 英尺到 75 000 英尺（可使用的空域限制）是超音速和高空飞行飞机使用的最高高度。

3. In most nations air traffic controllers who are stationed in air traffic control center are known as “area,” “en route, ” or, colloquially in the US, “center” controllers.

在大多数国家，驻扎在空中交通管制中心的空管人员被称为“区域”“进近”或者按照

美国的叫法，“中心”管制员。

Exercises

I. Analyze the following passages grammatically.

1. When the aircraft is safely separated and climbing in accordance with the standard instrument departure, it will be handed over to the first radar sector controller for his permission to climb to the cruising altitude.

2. The tower's airspace is often a 5-nautical-mile (9.3 km) radius around the airport, but can vary greatly in size and shape depending on traffic configuration and volume.

3. Communication is a vital part of the job: controllers are trained to focus on the exact words that pilots and other controllers speak, because a single misunderstanding about altitude levels or runway numbers can have tragic consequences.

II. Answer the following questions based on the text.

1. How is the interval between two take-off aircrafts regulated?
2. What are the three main high levels on the airways?
3. What does an air traffic controller do? What is the main task of the air traffic controller?
4. What is the default language of aviation worldwide?

Supplementary Reading Material

Which one is more stressful , air traffic controller or pilot?

Air traffic controller (ATC) and pilot have different schedule of work and both involve high levels of stress due to the vigilant nature of their work. Both pilots and ATC can have an early morning, afternoon, and night shift. According to Stoke (1994) employees have a higher level error rate from 3a.m. to 7a.m. and working this shift schedule can affect both psychological and physical health over the year. This researcher indicated that psychology and biochemical variables such as heart rate and temperature are different. The average heart rate is normal in an afternoon shift and a morning shift has higher levels of fairly normal circadian rhythm. In addition, stress could be higher from the morning shift because of higher levels of workload and the fatigue effect on human systems. However, the researchers have shown that for ATC and pilots, the night shift can have a significantly lower of workload. The night shift is the only shift associated with circadian rhythm disruption. Circadian rhythm affects on the human ability is slim during the night shift, but they're no guarantee that night shift can avoid the psychological stress. As a result, afternoon and night shift work has reduced stress at work than the morning shift. ATC position is more stressful because hours are larger, pay is lower and condition is larger responsibility with thousands of lives on the ground and in the air.

Key reasons ATC stressful than pilots:

- ATC work involves being responsible for tower control, radar control, weather observation, etc. As a result, ATC personnel have to balance workload, responsibility and recognition, and then it can be assumed that ATC job has potential of stress.
- According to Stokes (1994) ATC job has a high level of workplace stress, and effect to human health in the long term period. ATC has the ability to increase health problems from hypertension and peptic ulcers, more than pilots or office jobs.
- Overall, in the USA from 1972 to 1977 there were 79 ATC personnel disqualified from the ATC work and 61 were affected by psychological problems over the year they worked as ATC.
- However, ATC duty required 40 hours per week or more and some are on call on the duty, if the airport weather change such as fog, or thunders light, ATC duty is directly increased. This is more than pilots spends on the job and likely to increase stress.
- According to FAA (2012) average ATC salary received from $US32, 000 to $US166, 000. Due to lower pay rate, most ATC has significant problems with their finances while they're on the job.
- ATC has to go home and make their food and do the dishes after finish the meal compare to pilot professional and high quality foods.

Pilots working conditions

- According to NZ CAA Act 1990 a pilot is required to fly for 30 hours or 35hours for 2 pilots in any 7 consecutive days. Most commercial airlines required 2 or 3 pilots working in the cockpit during long haul flight. This shows that pilots have multiple crews on their duty to help reduce individual stress.
- Crew duty rest period requires 12 hours per day and crew duty maximum 11 hours per day.
- Pilots are required to have a meal every 4 or 6 hours during the flight period.
- During long haul flight, pilots use auto pilot to assist their performance. This means that individual pilot have owner assistance to reduce stress in the cockpit.
- Most pilots have higher salaries than ATC. According to FAA (2012) the average commercial airline pilots received US$110, 000 per year. This shows that most pilots may have less worry about their financial problems and therefore less stress.

In conclusion, the ATC is more stressful than the pilot because they have larger responsibility to control lives in the air and on the ground in the same time. Work hours, salary, foods, and workloads add to the daily stress of ATC.

资料来源：http://aviationknowledge.wikidot.com/sop:which-one-is-more-stressful-air-traffic-control-or-pilot

Unit Nine

The Control Tower

Text

Passage

The control tower is the nerve-centre of an airport. At the busiest international centres controllers may direct up to 2,000 aircrafts, movements a day, more than one a minute during the busiest hours.

The tower has to be tall enough to give controllers an unobstructed view across the airfield. It may be a small double-decker cabin at a club airfield from which one controller directs aircraft along a single airstrip, or as large as the 260-feet monolith at Charles de Gaulle Airport, from where a team of seven or more command a view across a runway complex of 11 square miles.

Control towers in the large airports have two control rooms. Controllers in the visual control room at the top are responsible for aircraft taking off for aircraft taxying, and for final landing instructions. Assistants log aircraft departure and arrival times, from which landing charges are prepared, and the computer, which prints out the estimated arrival time and scheduled departure time of each plane. A ground movement planning controller books slots (available times) along the airways for departures.

An atmosphere of cool urgency prevails in the dimly-lit approach control room, usually located below. Here, approach controllers, working in the orange glow from their radarscopes, guide inbound traffic to the runways. Should a runway inspection, or overloading at peak hours, cause a delay, aircrafts are fed into holding stacks, flying around a radio beacon until given landing clearance. The approach controllers integrate the flow from two or more stacks, handing them over to a radar director, who weaves the streams into a single line stretching out along the approach path. A safe separation distance of three to four miles between incoming flights provides a landing interval about one minute. Aircrafts overflying the congested airport zone are controlled by a separate radar direction.

The radar screens are ringed with concentric circles, called range marks, representing distances of two, five or ten miles from the antenna. With the aid of a compass rose super-imposed on the radarscope, controllers can accurately calculate aircraft positions. Dotted and solid lines encircle radio-navigation reference points. The "blips" or "targets" pinpoint each moving aircraft. In modern alphanumeric display, each target is labelled with the flight number, and the aircraft's altitude and routing, for rapid identification. The blip continually fades, then brightens as a new position appears.

Intense concentration is needed to track dozens of aircraft moving at speed within a small area, and controllers take a 30-minute "wind-down" break after a maximum of two hours' work on the radarscopes.

New words

1. unobstructed [ʌnəb'strʌktid]	adj. 没有障碍的，没有阻挡的
2. airstrip ['eəstrip]	n. 简易机场，简易跑道，飞机跑道
3. monolith ['mɒn(ə)liθ]	n. 整块石料，独块石料制品；庞然大物
4. slot [slɒt]	n. 飞机起降时间；缝隙；轨迹
5. atmosphere ['ætməsfiə]	n. 气氛，大气
6. prevail [pri'veil]	v. 胜（过），流行，盛行
7. glow [gləu]	n. 白热光，光辉
8. feed [fiːd]	v. 填；喂；供给
9. stack [stæk]	n. 令飞机分层盘旋飞行等待着陆
10. congest [kən'dʒest]	v. 拥挤；使密集
11. concentric [kən'sentrik]	adj. 同一中心的，同轴的
12. antenna [æn'tenə]	n. 天线
13. dot [dɒt]	v. 打点于，加点于
14. blip [blip]	n.（显示器屏幕上的）标志，反射脉冲尖头信号
15. target ['tɑːgit]	n. 目标，靶子
16. pinpoint ['pinpɔint]	v. 为……准确定位，指示，确认
17. alphanumeric [ˌælfənjuː'merik]	adj. 文字数字式的，字母数字的
18. concentration [kɔns(ə)n'treiʃ(ə)n]	n. 集中；全神贯注；浓缩

Phrases and expressions

1. control tower	塔台（管制台）
2. Charles De Gaulle Airport	戴高乐机场
3. landing instructions (clearance)	着陆指示（许可）
4. approach control room	进近管制室
5. peak hour	高峰时间
6. holding stacks	分层盘旋飞行，在空中等待着陆指示
7. incoming flights	进港飞机（航班）
8. range marks	距离指标
9. with the aid of	在……援助下，借助于
10. compass rose	方向刻度环（盘）
11. dotted and solid lines	虚线和实线

Abbreviations

1. ETA estimated times of arrival 预计到达时间
2. ETD estimated times of departure 预计起飞时间

Notes

1. An atmosphere of cool urgency prevails in the dimly-lit approach control room.
灯光暗淡的进近管制室中笼罩着一种冷静而紧迫的气氛。

2. ..., aircraft are fed into holding stacks, flying around a radio beacon until given landing clearance.
……，就将飞机安排在分层盘旋等待区，围绕无线电信标台飞行，直到发给着陆许可。

3. With the aid of a compass rose superimposed on the radarscope, ...
借助于雷达荧光屏上叠加的一个方向刻度盘，……

Exercises

I. Explain the following special terms and learn by heart.

1. Control Tower: A terminal facility which provides air traffic control (ATC) service to airborne aircraft operating in the vicinity of an airport.

2. Airway: A control area, or portion thereof established in the form of a corridor equipped with radio navigation aids.

3. Instrument Landing System: A precision instrument approach system designed to provide electronically a path for exact alignment and descent of an aircraft on final approach to a runway.

II. Try to practise some of instructions used by the ground control.

1. Ground control, Silverbird five-o-one on stand Juliet one-five requesting start-up clearance.

2. Silverbird five-o-one is cleared to the John E. Kennedy Airport. Your initial routing is to Brecon twelve.

3. Silverbird five-o-one requesting taxi clearance. Silverbird five-o-one taxi to R/W 28 left via the outer.

4. Listen out one-one-eight point seven for takeoff clearance.

5. Silverbird five-o-one hold short of the R/W.

6. Silverbird five-o-one is cleared to line up and take off. Wind 260 at 12.

7. Silverbird five-o-one now climb to six thousand feet. Change to one-one-nine point three.

III. Answer the following questions based on the text.

1. What is the nerve centre of an airport? How many aircraft may the controllers at the

busiest international centres direct a day?

2. In what area does a control tower operate?

3. What are the controllers in the visual control room at the top responsible for?

4. What do the approach controllers working in the orange glow from their radarscopes do?

5. Is intense concentration needed to track dozens of aircraft moving at speed within a small area?

Supplementary Reading Material

Control Tower Design

AERTEC Solutions, as an aeronautical engineering firm specialised in airport infrastructures, also has extensive experience in the design of what could be considered as the most recognisable of all aeronautical buildings – the airport control tower.

Our team of multidiscipline engineers is capable of taking on the design of buildings of this type with the utmost efficiency.

When it comes down to it, a control tower is just a building, however the way in which it is used is a factor that sets it apart from a standard building, giving it an extra dimension.

As a first step in the design of this type of building, AERTEC Solutions would typically create a planning and location study for the building, unless of course this is provided beforehand by the client. This type of study analyses the factors that must be taken into account when designing a facility with these characteristics.

One factor to take into account is that the control tower cab must have a clear view of all the most critical and furthest points of the airfield, along with all the flight paths in close proximity to the airport. Conversely, the control tower must not affect the obstacle limitation surfaces of the airport. These two conflicting requirements determine the minimum and maximum height of the building, which in turn helps establish the most suitable location for the tower.

As well as these two fundamental characteristics, other factors must be taken into account such as access to utilities networks, controlled access from landside, among others. After evaluating all of these different criteria, the preferred location will be determined. The building can then be equipped with all the required equipment to correctly operate, recognising the client's budget.

Once the location for the building has been chosen, the design concept is created. A basic programme for surface areas will be developed, in which the height and type of use for the building must be agreed between the developers and the operators that will be using it. Obviously, the cab of the control tower is the most recognisable part, with all the other elements being based around it. Usually located below the cab are the auxiliary services rooms, containing elements that support the cab. This includes the navigation equipment, communications and AGL equipment, along with technical rooms and rest areas for the air traffic controllers. In addition, the air-conditioning equipment must also be located as close to the cab as possible, however it is important that the cab is not affected by noise or vibration.

AERTEC Solutions would also perform a study of the wind effects on the building, which may include wind tunnel simulations.

According to the specific needs of each client, other services, such as meteorological services, can be located close to the cab.

Once the different elements that are required to be located close to the cab have been decided, all others will then be located at the base of the shaft, therefore reducing costs.

Airport control towers, by design, are slender buildings. They must allow the controllers to work without any interference from noise or vibration. With this in mind, AERTEC Solutions pays special attention to the stability of the building and possible effects from seismic activity or wind. As well as performing the structural analysis required for this type of building, AERTEC Solutions would also carry out a wind turbulence assessment.

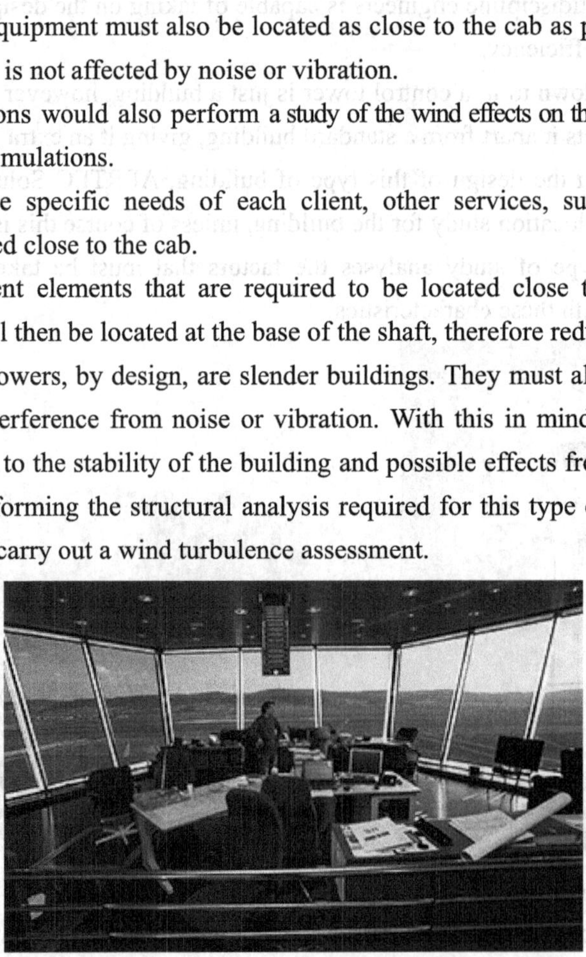

In terms of the building's installations, the fact that it provides air navigation services means that additional care must be taken regarding a series of factors that directly affect the availability of this service. For example, the air conditioning both for the cab and for the navigation and communications equipment must be sufficient for needs and also be equipped with an alternative power supply. The electrical installation must also operate correctly, protecting the facility and the people that use it, while also being robust and reliable.

Finally, it must always be remembered that air traffic controllers are people, therefore the building must comply with health & safety and fire prevention requirements. AERTEC Solutions are fully aware of all the issues that typically arise in this type of building. To tackle these potential issues head-on, at the start of the project AERTEC Solutions ensure that two key elements are covered. Firstly we make sure that all relevant standards are complied with and secondly we ensure that correct communication channels are established between air traffic control representatives and airport fire & rescue services. This ensures that all their requirements are covered in the project.

资料来源：http://www.aertecsolutions.com/aviation/control-towers-design/?lang=en

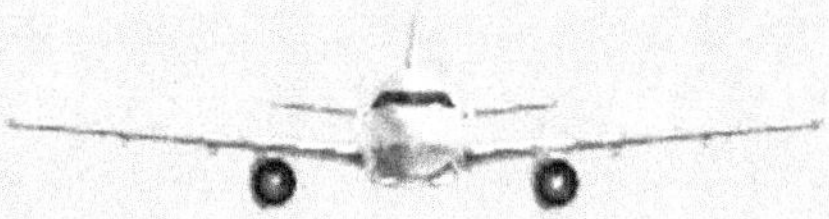

Unit Ten
Flight Planning

Text

Passage

Prior to each departure of an aircraft, a pilot or flight dispatcher has to file flight plans with the local Civil Aviation Authority, which are crucial documents indicating the plane's planned route or flight path. The old-fashioned flight planning room in which pilots study charts and other documents on long tables has been replaced by a modernized office equipped with various electronic devices these days where flights are usually dispatched in less than half an hour.

Flight crew checks in an hour or so before a flight. Some airline crews will work in teams since they always fly together and know each other very well. In some cases, the crew members may not have met each other before. A stand-in may be called if anyone is absent.

Critical data about the aircraft itself, departure and arrival points, payload of passengers, freight, luggage and fuel, latest weather changes en route and at the destination will be typed into a computer and several possible optimized routes will be printed out (minimum distance, minimum time, minimum cost). Then the best one is selected. Usually the routes are allocated on "first come, first served" for flight crews if they want the same route.

Airplanes fly along designated airways, which can be thought of as three-dimensional highways for aircraft. But they do not necessarily link two cities. The aircraft follow radio beams sent by the ground stations. Most airways are eight nautical miles (14 kilometers) wide, and the airway flight levels keep aircraft separated by at least 1,000 vertical feet from aircraft on the flight level above and below. They usually intersect at NAVAIDs, which designate the allowed points for changing from one airway to another. Airways have names consisting of one or more letters followed by one or more digits such as R342 or G17. Pilots follow these tracks from one station to another, but may make a detour due to bad weather en route.

Pilots who plan long-distance flight may adopt great circle route, which is the shortest distance between departure point and destination, especially when no airway links the two points. Despite the difficulty, modern navigation systems make this possible.

Calculation of fuel requirements is the most safety-critical aspect of flight planning. This calculation is somewhat complicated since it must take many factors into account like route choice, weather forecast, and the weight of airplane and so on. Generally, the heavier the aircraft is, the higher the fuel consumption rate will be. Since the weight of fuel forms a significant part of the total weight of an aircraft, it also costs fuel to carry fuel. Apart from the amount of fuel carried to the destination, a contingency amount should also be taken into account in case of diversion, holding, headwind and other emergency situations in order to ensure flight safety. It would be a silly idea to carry maximum fuel before each flight especially if the flight is short or the aircraft takes off or lands on short runways. What's more, the cost of fuel is also an important consideration for airlines. However, due to the varied prices in different places, it is also reasonable to load up with cheap fuel and burn extra to avoid filling up where fuel is costly.

Sheets of navigation and weather data, notices of conditions at destination and alternate airports, lists of VIPs and CIPs, details of passengers' special requirements as well as the flight plan constitute a great document which needs to be signed by the captain for acceptance and confirmed by the dispatcher. Then the document, together with lists of emergency equipment and procedures, will be submitted to the national air traffic control service. Copies are teleprinted out to the control centres along the route. With the authorized data, the flight crew leaves for the aircraft.

New words

1. dispatcher [dɪs'pætʃə]	n. 签派员，调度员；调度程序
2. indicate ['ɪndɪkeɪt]	v. 表明，指出；预示；象征
3. stand-in ['stændin]	n. 替身
4. payload ['peɪləʊd]	n. 有效负荷
5. freight [freɪt]	n. 货运；运费；船货
	v. 运送；装货；使充满
6. optimized ['ɔptimaizd]	adj. 最佳化的；尽量充分利用
7. three-dimensional ['θri:dɪ'menʃənəl]	adj. 三维的；立体的；真实的
8. vertical ['vɜ:tɪk(ə)l]	n. 垂直的，垂直面；垂直位置
	adj. 垂直的，直立的；顶点的
9. intersect [ɪntə'sekt]	v. 横断，横切；贯穿
10. designate ['dezɪgneɪt]	v. 指定；指派；标出；把……定名为
	adj. 指定的；选定的
11. detour ['di:tʊə]	v. 使……绕道而行；迂回
	n. 绕道；便道
12. calculation [kælkjʊ'leɪʃ(ə)n]	n. 计算；估算；计算的结果
13. contingency [kən'tɪndʒ(ə)nsɪ]	n. 偶然性；意外事故；意外开支
14. diversion [daɪ'vɜ:ʃ(ə)n]	n. 转移；消遣；分散注意力
15. holding ['həʊldɪŋ]	n. 举办；支持
	v. 召开；担任；握住
16. headwind ['hɛdwɪnd]	n. 逆风；顶头风
17. constitute ['kɒnstɪtju:t]	v. 组成，构成；建立；任命
18. teleprint ['telɪprɪt]	n. 电传打字机；电传打印机

Phrases and expressions

1. flight planning 飞行计划
2. prior to 在……之前
3. electronic device 电子仪表，电子设施
4. flight crew 机组人员
5. en route 航路上
6. radio beam 无线电波束
7. great circle route 大圆圈航线
8. fuel consumption rate 耗油率
9. alternate airport 备降机场

Abbreviations

1. VIP very important person (passenger) 重要任务，要人（重要乘客）
2. CIP commercially important people 商界重要人士

Notes

1. Pilots follow these tracks from one station to another, but may make a detour due to bad weather en route.

飞行员由一个导航台飞向另一个导航台，但有时也会因为航路上的恶劣天气而选择绕飞。

2. Since the weight of fuel forms a significant part of the total weight of an aircraft, it also costs fuel to carry fuel.

由于燃油本身也是飞机总重的一部分，因此载油的同时也会耗油。

3. However, due to the varied prices in different places, it is also reasonable to load up with cheap fuel and burn extra to avoid filling up where fuel is costly.

然而，由于各地油价不同，为避免在油价高的地方加油，选择在油价便宜的地方加满油并在航路上消耗多余的燃油也是合理的。

Exercises

I. Write down the full name of each abbreviation and translate it into Chinese.

1. VFR
2. IFR
3. NOTAM
4. WBM
5. VMC
6. IMC

7. AFIS
8. AIS
9. AWS
10. CARs

II. Try to explain the following terms with the help of dictionary.

1. payload
2. operating weight empty
3. zero fuel weight
4. ramp weight
5. brake release weight
6. takeoff weight
7. landing weight

III. Read and translate the following short passages into Chinese.

1. In recent years, renewable energy resources have become more important due to the limited number of regions for production of petroleum-based fuels, which are continuously depleting. The aviation sector in terms of commercial and cargo transportation has an increasing need for conventional, as well as alternative fuels. Derivatives of petroleum fuels used in aviation have negative impacts on air quality. Factors causing greenhouse gas emissions (GHG) in the aviation sector must be reduced. Biofuels which are already used for ground vehicles could also be implemented in the aviation sector to reduce fuel cost and emissions and to help with sustainability and a better environment.

2. In general, flight planners are expected to avoid areas called Special Use Airspace (SUA) when planning a flight. SUA is an area designated for operations of a certain nature that an aircraft is restricted to get involved in. These operations are usually of military nature. Most SUAs are depicted on aeronautical charts. There are several types of SUAs, including restricted airspace, prohibited airspace, military operations area (MOA), warning areas, alert areas, temporary flight restriction (TFR), national security areas and controlled firing areas. Examples of such airspace include a region around the White House in Washington D.C. and the country of Cuba.

3. Part of flight planning often involves the identification of one or more airports which can be flown to in case of unexpected condition (such as weather) at the destination airport. The planning process must be careful to include only alternative airports which can be reached with the anticipated fuel load and total aircraft weight and which have capabilities necessary to handle the type of aircraft being flown. What's more, holding over the destination or alternative airports due to unexpected weather or congestion is also an important consideration for flight planning. If the flight plan calls for hold planning, the additional fuel and hold time should also appear on the

flight plan.

IV. Answer the following questions based on the text.

1. Where are flights dispatched? And how long are flights dispatched?

2. How do people get an ideal route for an airliner?

3. How do you understand airways? Do they link cities?

4. Is it possible for an airplane to carry the amount of fuel just enough to the destination as a way of saving fuel?

5. What constitute the document signed by the captain for acceptance before flight?

Supplementary Reading Material

How to Plan a VFR Cross Country Flight

Planning a cross-country flight can seem like a daunting task. Here's a step-by-step process to make VFR flight planning a bit easier.

Choose Your Destination

Choosing a destination is easy, for the most part. Much of the time, pilots choose to fly to the airports with the best restaurants and best service. There are some other things to consider, though. As a student, you'll likely have certain lesson requirements to accomplish.

Another thing to keep in mind is the services at your destination. Make sure fuel is available if you need it. And once you have a destination in mind, get a weather briefing and NOTAMs before you continue to ensure you won't run into bad weather or a closed runway.

Choose Your Route

Choose a route that will allow you to fly at a safe optimum altitude for your aircraft while still allowing you to easily identify checkpoints on the ground. If you're going to navigate with the help of instruments, you can choose routes that go to and from VORs.

Choose checkpoints that are 5-10 nautical miles apart and easy to identify. Lakes, rivers, towns and other airports are usually easy to spot. Over very flat land with less-than-ideal checkpoints, you might need to fly an indirect route to make sure you don't get lost. Once you choose your route, plot it out on a VFR sectional map.

Get a Weather Briefing

There are a variety of different ways you can obtain weather information.

The first and possibly most popular option is to call the flight service station. Calling the number 1-800-WX-BRIEF will put you in touch with an air traffic control specialist that is FAA-certified as a Pilot Weather Briefer.

The second option is to use CSC DUATS or DTC DUATS, each of which offers FAA-approved weather information. DUATS systems offer an abundance of weather information, flight planning tools and the option to file a flight plan.

Finally, pilots can use any of the widely-used sources for weather information, as long as they can be considered reliable. Stick to NOAA, airport weather observation reports, and pilot reports.

Choose an Altitude and Cruise Profile

You'll want to fly high enough to maintain the required clearance from terrain and obstacles, of course, but you'll want to consider aircraft performance and the ability to find checkpoints from the air, as well.

The performance charts in the pilot operating handbook or pilot information manual for your aircraft can help you determine an altitude and cruise power setting to use to get the best range or best endurance.

Compute Airspeed, Time and Distance

You'll need to complete the speed, distance, and time for each leg of the flight, as well as fuel consumption. It's easiest to follow a navigation log form for this. You can do it by hand or use a trusted computer or iPad application like ForeFlight.

Using a navigation log can help you organize the calculations in a way that makes sense and easy to use.

Familiarize Yourself With the Airport

If you've ever been stuck at a busy airport without an airport diagram, then you know that it's imperative to keep your situational awareness_even after you land. Taxi instructions can be lengthy and you'll want to know what you're doing when you're surrounded by Boeing 737s and MD-80s.

Besides getting familiar with the airport layout, you should know which FBO to use and the hours of operation. You'll want to make sure fuel and other services are available when you need them. Besides, you'll probably need a restroom.

Double-Check Your Equipment

If you're reliant on certain navigational instruments, make sure they work. Ensure the GPS database is up to date and working, and make sure the VOT check has been done to ensure the VOR system is reliable.

Make sure you are equipped with survival gear, appropriate clothing for the weather, flashlights, charts, and water. And don't forget to charge your iPad.

Get an Updated Briefing

For most, it takes a few hours to get everything prepared for a cross-country flight. Weather can change quickly and airports can close unexpectedly, so be sure to call the flight service station for an abbreviated briefing. If the winds have changed, you may want to make a few adjustments to your speed and time calculations before you depart.

File a Flight Plan

After you get your weather briefing from the flight service specialist, you'll want to file a flight plan. Filing a flight plan with the flight service station adds a layer of safety; if you don't show up to close the flight plan, and you can't otherwise be found at your destination, search and rescue will be alerted — which means you'll need to remember to close your flight plan when you arrive safely!

Be Prepared for the Unexpected

A flight plan makes cross-country flying a breeze. But as everyone knows, sometimes things don't go as planned. Be prepared mentally to adjust your plans as necessary. If your VOR fails, you might need to rely more heavily on your map reading skills. And if the weather deteriorates, you may need to divert to a different airport.

If you plan for the unexpected, you'll be ready for anything.

资料来源：https://www.thebalancecareers.com/how-to-plan-a-vfr-cross-country-flight-282900

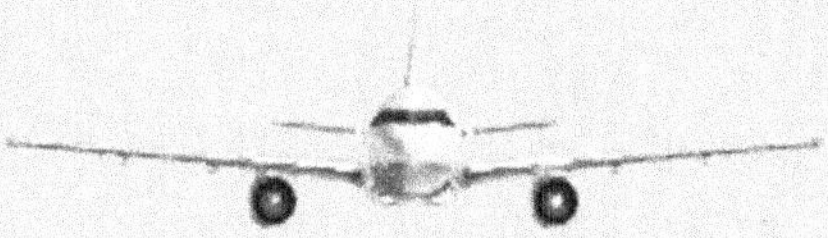

Unit Eleven
Weather Forecasting

Text

Passage

The smooth and safe operation of each flight is inseparable from the detailed meteorological data provided by the airport weather office. Before daybreak the duty forecasters go into a highly stressful state of gathering and studying weather data that has been following in all night from weather stations on land, at sea, in outer space, and from pilots in flight. After full digestion by the computer, the weather data is notified to the airline pilots in the form of code, which gives as detailed information as possible so that the pilots can determine if the weather is suitable for flying according to air regulations.

Airline pilots must familiarize themselves with the expected conditions for departure before take off. Fog now becomes a chief dreaded weather that may cause to boring delays. It is particularly annoying for the pilots when the fog pervades over the airport only while it is clear 1,000 feet up. In that case, they need to know when it will clear and whether it may come back. Fog often occurs when moist air passes over a cool surface by advection (wind) and is cooled. It is common as a warm front passes over an area with significant snow-pack. It is most common at sea when moist air encounters cooler waters, including areas of cold water upwelling. A strong enough temperature difference over water or bare ground can also cause it. Icing occurs in very humid air slightly below the freezing point, and the aircraft de-ice the wings with the hot air from jet engines during take off. This will reduce the take off power, so it may be necessary to adjust the load.

Pilots also need to know surface conditions of airports within 30-minute flying time. In case of engine failure after take off, the pilot may need to find a local alternate airport. Terminal aerodrome forecasts (TAFs) are complied at large airport weather office by meteorologists who know local weather patterns well.

Forecasters draw synoptic charts all day and constantly update them. Synoptic charts give the general weather picture for the surface and for high altitudes as well, through which the pilots are warned about deep depressions and winds around. When the aircraft encounter headwinds over one side of a depression, they consume more fuel. However, tailwinds on the other side not only shorten flight time but also cut down fuel consumption. The jet stream is a very strong wind that blows high in the earth's atmosphere and has an important influence on the weather. Meteorologists use the location of some of the jet streams as an aid in weather forecasting. The main commercial relevance of the jet streams is in air travel, as flight time can be dramatically affected by either flying with the flow or against, which results in significant fuel and time cost savings for airlines. Often, the airlines work to fly with the jet stream for this reason. Dynamic North Atlantic Tracks are one example of how airlines and air traffic control work together to accommodate the jet stream and winds aloft that results in the maximum benefit for airlines and other users.

Significant weather reports are one of the important references for aircraft fuel calculation. They may warn the pilots of thunderstorms which are usually accompanied by strong winds, heavy rain, and sometimes snow, sleet, hail, or, in contrast, no precipitation at all. Thunderstorms result from the rapid upward movement of warm, moist air, sometimes along a front. When thunderstorms rumble over a terminal airport, the aircraft has to land in the turbulence and sharp wind shear under massive thunderheads. Unfavorable wind shear may dangerously reduce the aircraft's speed by more than 60mph, so forecasters have to pay close attention to it.

Sometimes, the aircraft may encounter a special kind of cobblestone-like turbulence even in clear sky. Clear-air turbulence (CAT) is the turbulent movement of air masses in the absence of any visual clues such as clouds, and is caused when bodies of air moving at widely different speeds meet. Severe CAT may cause the aircraft to shake obviously and even change altitude, however it does not last long if the pilot could alter flight level. On May 1, 2017, Boeing 777 flight SU270 from Moscow to Thailand got into clear air turbulence. The aircraft suddenly dropped and 27 passengers who were not buckled up sustained serious injuries. The pilots were able to stabilize the plane and continue the flight. All passengers who needed medical attention were taken to Bangkok hospital upon arrival.

During the flight, the crew need to keep listening to sustained VHF air weather radio and keep watch on the aircraft's weather radar. In the event of a storm, they have to try their best to fly over or round it. Lightning in a storm does not cause structural damage to the aircraft, but it can burn the aerial or interfere with the radio navigation equipment, especially at a lower altitude. Hail is one of the most significant storm hazards to aircraft. When hail stones exceed 0.5 inches (13 mm) in diameter, planes can be seriously damaged within seconds. Wind shear is also monitored by the crew through inertial navigation equipment.

The weather is without national boundaries. Faced with all kinds of weather information and data, airline pilots do not need worry about difficulties in translation, because meteorologists have developed a universal meteorological language.

New words

1. meteorological [ˌmiːtɪərə'lɒdʒɪkl] adj. 气象的；气象学的
2. digestion [daɪ'dʒestʃ(ə)n] n. 消化；领悟；消化能力
3. dreaded ['dredɪd] adj. 令人畏惧的，害怕的

4. pervade [pə'veɪd] vt. 遍及，弥漫；渗透，充满
5. moist [mɔɪst] adj. 潮湿的；微湿的；多雨的
6. advection [æd'vɛkʃən] n. 移流；水平对流
7. upwell [ʌp'wel] vi.（水等）上涌
8. humid ['hju:mɪd] adj. 潮湿的；湿润的；湿气重的
9. meteorologist [ˌmi:tiə'rɒlədʒɪst] n. 气象学者
10. synoptic [sɪ'nɒptɪk] n. 天气学；气象图
11. depression [dɪˈpreʃ(ə)n] n. 低气压；沮丧；抑郁症
12. headwind ['hɛdwɪnd] n. 逆风；顶头风
13. tailwind ['teɪlwɪnd] n. 顺风
14. aloft [ə'lɒft] adv. 在高处；在空中
15. thunderstorm ['èʌndəstɔ:m] n. 大雷雨；雷电交加的暴风雨；雷暴
16. sleet [sli:t] n. 雨夹雪或雹
17. hail [heɪl] n. 冰雹
18. turbulence ['tɜ:bjul(ə)ns] n.（空气和水的）湍流，涡流，紊流
19. cobblestone ['kɒbl, stəun] n. 圆石，鹅卵石
20. aerial ['eəriəl] adj. 航空的，空中的
21. inertial [ɪ'nɜ:ʃl] adj. 惯性的；不活泼的
22. navigation [ˌnævɪ'geɪʃ(ə)n] n. 导航；领航

Phrases and expressions

1. duty forecaster 气象预报值班员
2. outer space 外层空间
3. freezing point 冰点
4. alternate airport 备降机场
5. synoptic chart 天气图
6. jet stream 急流
7. wind shear 风切（变）
8. flight level 飞行高度
9. weather radar 天气雷达
10. radio navigation equipment 无线电导航设备
11. inertial navigation equipment 惯性导航设备

Abbreviations

1. TAF terminal aerodrome forecast 终点机场天气预报
2. CAT clear-air turbulence 晴空大气扰流，晴空湍流
3. VHF very high frequency 甚高频

Notes

1. Fog now becomes a chief dreaded weather that may cause to boring delays. It is particularly annoying for the pilots when the fog pervades over the airport only while it is clear 1,000 feet up.

雾现在已经成为导致令人厌烦的飞机延误的罪魁祸首。当雾在机场上空弥漫而在 1 000 英尺以上时，尤其令飞行员恼火。

2. Icing occurs in very humid air slightly below the freezing point, and the aircraft de-ice the wings with the hot air from jet engines during takeoff.

结冰发生在稍低于冰点的潮湿空气中，飞机在起飞时用喷气发动机的热气给机翼除冰。

3. On May 1, 2017, Boeing 777 flight SU270 from Moscow to Thailand got into clear air turbulence. The aircraft suddenly dropped and 27 passengers who were not buckled up sustained serious injuries.

2017 年 5 月 1 日，一架航班号是 SU270 的波音 777 飞机在从莫斯科飞往泰国的途中遭遇晴空湍流，飞机突然下降，机上 27 名乘客因未扣好安全带而受重伤。

Exercises

I. Translate the following phrases into Chinese.

1. aeronautical meteorology
2. aviation meteorological observation
3. aviation area (weather) forecast
4. aviation meteorological information
5. aeronautical climate regionalization
6. airplane meteorological sounding
7. significant meteorological information
8. hazardous weather message
9. aerodrome hazardous weather warning
10. ICAO standard atmosphere
11. flight visibility
12. runway visual range
13. icing on runway
14. meteorological minimum
15. aerodrome meteorological minimum
16. unflyable weather
17. plain-language report
18. aviation meteorological code

19. pilot meteorological report
20. aviation meteorological support
21. appointed airdrome weather report
22. aircraft weather reconnaissance
23. VOLMET broadcast
24. aviation (weather) forecast
25. air route (weather) forecast
26. amendment of aviation weather forecast
27. landing (weather) forecast
28. aerodrome special weather report
29. altimeter setting
30. aircraft icing
31. clear air turbulence, CAT
32. aircraft bumpiness
33. aircraft trail
34. (exhaust) contrail
35. (exhaust) evaporation trail
36. aircraft wake
37. low-level wind shear
38. airdrome pressure
39. tail wind
40. cross wind
41. head wind
42. navigation wind
43. wind sleeve

II. Analyze the following passages grammatically.

1. Before daybreak the duty forecasters go into a highly stressful state of gathering and studying weather data that has been following in all night from weather stations on land, at sea, in outer space, and from pilots in flight.

2. The main commercial relevance of the jet streams is in air travel, as flight time can be dramatically affected by either flying with the flow or against, which results in significant fuel and time cost savings for airlines.

3. Lightning in a storm does not cause structural damage to the aircraft, but it can burn the aerial or interfere with the radio navigation equipment, especially at a lower altitude.

III. Answer the following questions based on the text.

1. How do the aircraft de-ice the wings?

2. Who makes terminal aerodrome forecasts?
3. What are thunderstorms usually accompanied by?
4. Why do the forecasters have to pay close attention to unfavorable wind shear?
5. What is clear-air turbulence?

Supplementary Reading Material

How Pilots Avoid Thunderstorms

With its clear skies, sunshine, and warm temperatures, Florida is one of the best locations out there when it comes to flight training. But clear skies are often a product of unstable air, which makes Florida a hot spot for thunderstorm activity in the summer. And an airplane is no match for a thunderstorm. Pilots must take action to avoid thunderstorms, which can be challenging, especially during the summer months. How do they do it? Here are a few ways.

1. Preflight Planning

Thunderstorm avoidance is mostly accomplished during the early planning stage of a flight. The first thing a pilot will do during the planning process is check the weather by watching the news or looking at weather websites. As the departure time gets closer, the pilot will plan his or her flight using weather data from official weather sources like www.aviationweather.gov or one of the popular iPad apps like ForeFlight. Pilots have fantastic forecasting tools and weather reports available that allow them to see and predict thunderstorm activity. If the proposed route of flight goes through thunderstorm activity or there is thunderstorm activity forecasted for the flight path, the route will be altered, either around the thunderstorm or in a different direction. Flying through a thunderstorm is just not an option.

The second part of the planning process involves calling a Flight Service station to get a weather briefing. The flight service specialist is trained to provide the pilot with a comprehensive weather briefing and other information for their route of flight. The briefer will give the pilot a "big picture" view of the weather in the area as well as reported and forecast conditions at the departure and destination airports. This allows the pilot to make the best decision about their route of flight, including which areas they may want to avoid and which airports might be good alternates if bad weather prevents them from landing at their destination.

2. In-Flight Weather Services

During training, flights might be cancelled often due to thunderstorms. After all, the risk is just not worth the reward. But in the real world, corporate and airline pilots are tasked with getting their passengers where they need to go and they will often go to great lengths to plan flights around thunderstorms. And sometimes, pilots will just depart, knowing that they'll need to circumnavigate a storm or two in order to get to their destination. To do this, they use a variety of inflight tools such as a service called Hazardous Inflight Weather Advisory Service (HIWAS) and En Route Flight Advisory Services (EFAS) as well as the many digital weather products available today via iPads and other tablets. This information gives pilots updated and real-time information about thunderstorm activity.

3. Air Traffic Controllers

Pilots and controllers work together to ensure everyone gets where they need to go safely, and avoiding thunderstorms is no exception. Air traffic controllers will advise pilots on weather conditions when warranted, and pilots can often be heard requesting updated weather conditions from controllers, or requesting deviations to avoid thunderstorms when necessary. A pilot is ultimately responsible for not flying into a thunderstorm, so prompt communication with ATC is necessary to avoid them when the proposed route of flight takes a pilot into a storm. Pilots often use ATC as a resource, since controllers on the ground often have access to more up-to-date weather sources than pilots do.

4. Weather Radar Technology

These days, digital onboard technology is a helpful resource for pilots that fly technologically advanced aircraft. Aircraft with modernized avionics will often have weather radar systems, which gives pilots a graphic display of the location and intensity of thunderstorm activity and precipitation. Airborne weather radar is a great tool for thunderstorm avoidance, but it has disadvantages and shouldn't be relied upon as a sole means of detecting storms.

5. See And Avoid

One of the easiest and most common methods for detecting summer thunderstorms is the see-and-avoid method, which just means that a pilot shouldn't fly into a thunderstorm. This works in locations where thunderstorms are surrounded by clear skies, but sometimes thunderstorms are embedded in cloud layers, making them difficult to see. Embedded thunderstorms are especially dangerous for pilots traveling long distances, and a reason it's so important for pilots to get a preflight briefing.

6. Divert

Even the best preflight planning and onboard weather radar won't move a storm system out of the way, so there are times when a pilot must divert to an alternate airport. Diversions are rare, but are sometimes the only option when storm systems are unpredictable or widespread.

资料来源：https://www.pea.com/blog/posts/pilots-avoid-thunderstorms/

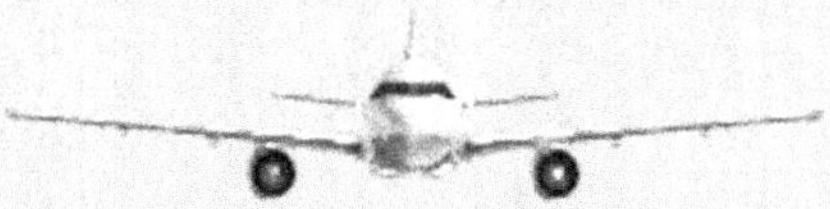

Unit Twelve

Emergencies

Text

Passage

Accidents do happen, and when they do, crew training, aircraft equipments and the good sense of the passengers may be fundamental to survival. To be alert to (but not obsessed with) the possibility of an emergency increases the chance of survival.

Aircraft seat belts, like the seats, are designed to withstand sudden deceleration. Work out how to fasten and unfasten them quickly. Cabin crews check that they are fastened at take off and landing, and that babies are installed in special cot-holders.

Do not, unless you are well versed in them, ignore the safety demonstrations at the beginning of a flight. Learn how to put on a lifejacket, and how to use the emergency oxygen masks stored above the seat or in the back of the seat in front: to cope withe sudden high altitude decompression, there will be very little time to find out how to put them on. Each magazine in pocket has a card of safety instructions. It gives the positions of the emergency exits. Each of these has a sign giving the operating instructions in one or more languages, so they can be opened by passengers.

Fire extinguishers and sometimes axes are stowed at the cabin crew stations. Life raft stowages are usually near each main exit; in wide-bodied jets they are extensions of the escape slides, and in aircraft such as the VC10, 707 and 747 they are stored in the ceiling above the isle. The survival, first-aid polar kites is usually found near, perhaps attached to, the life rafts or exits.

If the "fasten seats belts" signs flash on in flight, obey them quickly; the aircraft may be about to enter turbulence and passengers walking about, especially at the back, could be thrown around.

Extinguish cigarettes immediately the "no smoking" signs go on (in the ashtray, never on the floor). Never smoke in the toilets where inflammable materials are invariably used in the furnishings. Between 1946 and 1976, 316 accidents were caused by in-flight fires or smoke: many began in the toilets.

In an emergency, obey the cabin crew without questions. They will order passengers to fasten seat belts, extinguish cigarettes and brace themselves (bracing positions are illustrated on the "safety instructions" card) for sudden deceleration. They manage the exits when the aircraft stops, instruct passengers to evacuate on the procedure, and collect emergency equipment and supplies. If doors are inoperative, they activate the emergency exits, ordering passengers to unfasten seat belts, leave everything behind, and make for the designated escape chutes indicated by the cabin staff.

At the doorway, jump or slide down the chute to the ground (or into the life raft). Then get away from the aircraft. Move fast, and forget your belongings. In a fire, stragglers may be overcome by toxic fumes released by burning cabin furnishings.

New words

1. accident ['æksidənt]	n. 事故
2. fundamental [ˌfʌndə'mɛntl]	adj. 根本的，基础的
3. obsess [əb'ses]	v. 缠住，使烦扰
4. withstand [wið'stænd]	v. 经受住，抵挡，顶得住
5. deceleration ['diːˌselə'reiʃən]	n. 减速
6. install [in'stɔːl]	v. 安置，安装
7. cot [kɒt]	n. 儿童摇床，帆布床
8. versed [vɜːst]	adj. 精通的，通晓的；熟练的
9. ignore [ig'nɔː]	v. 轻视，忽视，不顾
10. mask [mɑːsk]	n. 面具，面罩
11. depressurization [diːˌpreʃərai'zeiʃən]	n. 减压，降压
12. extinguisher [ik'stiŋgwiʃə]	n. 灭火器
13. raft [ræft]	n. 木筏，筏子
14. polar ['pəulə]	adj. 地极的，极性的
15. ashtray ['æʃtrei]	n. 烟灰碟
16. inflammable [in'flæməbl]	adj. 易燃的，易着（火）的
17. brace [breis]	v. 拉紧，系紧，支住
18. illustrate ['iləstreit]	v.（用图）说明
19. man [mæn]	v. 操纵，守住，给…配备人员
20. inoperative [in'ɒp(ə)rətiv]	adj. 不起作用的，不工作的；无效力的
21. activate ['æktiveit]	v. 使活动，使活化
22. chute [ʃuːt]	n. 斜道，滑梯，降落伞
23. straggler ['strægələ]	n. 落伍者，掉队者，散乱跑动者
24. toxic ['tɒksik]	adj. 有毒的，有毒气的；中毒的
25. fume [fjuːm]	n. 烟，气，汽；愤怒；烦恼
26. release [ri'liːs]	v. 释放；发射；散发 n. 释放；发布；让与
27. furnishings ['fəːniʃiŋz]	n. 家具；设备；穿戴用品

Phrases and expressions

1. safety demonstrations(instructions)	安全示范（指示）

2. emergency oxygen mask 紧急氧气面罩
3. fire extinguisher 灭火器
4. escape slide (chute) 紧急离机滑板，逃生滑梯
5. first-aid kit 急救箱
6. inflammable materials 易燃品

Notes

1. To be alert to (but not obsessed with) the possibility of an emergency increases the chance of survival.

对发生紧急情况的可能性要有所警惕（但不要过于担心）才能增加幸存的机会。

2. …to cope with sudden high altitude decompression…

……如果在高空突然发生机舱失压……

3. In an emergency, obey the cabin crew without questions.

在发生紧急情况时，要毫无疑问地听从乘务人员的指挥。

Exercises

I. Read the explanations of the emergency instructions.

1. How to use life vest

When instructed by crew, put arms through loops, then place jacket over head, grasp straps under arms, pull down front and back. Pull tab-end straps in outward motion until jacket is snug. Do not inflate jacket inside the cabin.

2. How to use escape slide

For rapid escape to the ground, a special slide is installed at each cabin door exit. All crew members know how to use the slides. Obey their instructions.

3. How to use emergency exit

Window exits are in the middle of the cabin leading onto the wings. To unlock and open, pull handle above window. A life line, located in top of exit, attaches to ring on top of wing for assistance in leaving airport.

II. Try to practise the following emergency communication procedure.

Mayday[3]. This is PK759[3], on 5674 kilocycles. Position eight two kilometres sounth of London. True heading two seven zero, speed two zero zero knots, altitude eight thousand feet. Engine failure. Ditching. PK 759. Over.

III. Answer the following questions based on the text.

1. What are the fundamentals to survival if accident happens?
2. Do the cabin crews check that the seat belts are fastened at takeoff and landing and that

babies are installed in special cot-holders?

3. Have you learned how to put on a life jacket and how to use the emergency oxygen masks in accordance with safety demonstrations at the beginning of a flight?

4. Do you smoke in the toilet of the plane? How many accidents were there caused by in-flight fires or smoke in which many were begun in the toilets between 1946 and 1976?

5. What are the cabin crew going to do if doors are inoperative?

Supplementary Reading Material

Mother of two dies in mid-air crisis after being wedged in Southwest plane window

news of *USA today*, April 17, 2018

Shrapnel from a blown jet engine crashed through a window of a Southwest Airlines flight and caused such a perilous drop in air pressure that a passenger suffered fatal injuries after nearly being sucked outside.

Passengers recall a harrowing scene where desperate crew members and others tried to plug the broken window, while also trying to save the mortally wounded woman, identified as a bank executive and mother of two.

The battered jet eventually made an emergency landing in Philadelphia and all other passengers made it off without serious injuries. But not before everyone on board used oxygen masks that dropped from the ceiling and many said their prayers and braced for impact.

"I just remember holding my husband's hand, and we just prayed and prayed and prayed," said passenger Amanda Bourman, of New York. "And the thoughts that were going through my head of course were about my daughters, just wanting to see them again and give them a big hug so they wouldn't grow up without parents."

Dallas-bound Southwest Airlines Flight 1380 out of New York had 144 passengers and a crew of five onboard, Southwest said in a statement. The plane was met on the tarmac by a phalanx of emergency vehicles that quickly sprayed the area with safety foam and aided the injured.

Jennifer Riordan of Albuquerque, N.M., was identified late Tuesday as the victim who died.

Riordan, a vice president of community relations for Wells Fargo bank and graduate of the University of New Mexico, was the first passenger death on a US airline since 2009— and the first ever in Southwest Airlines' history.

New Mexico Gov. Susana Martinez called Riordan "an incredible woman who put her family and community first" and said her loss would be felt across the state.

"The hearts of all New Mexicans are with the Riordan family," Martinez, a Republican, said in a statement on Tuesday.

Passengers on board described chaos as the decompression led to Riordan being partially sucked out of the plane. They rushed to try and pull her back inside but her injuries were too grave.

Seven others were injured in the incident. Tracking data from FlightAware.com showed Flight 1380 was heading west over Pennsylvania at about 32,200 feet and traveling 500 mph when it abruptly turned toward Philadelphia.

National Transportation Safety Board Chairman Robert Sumwalt told reporters at a late-night briefing that he is "very concerned" about metal fatigue in several of Flight 1380's jet engines, particularly in the fan blades. He said a piece of one of the jet engines was found about 70 miles north of the Philadelphia airport.

Bourman was asleep on the plane when she heard a sudden noise and the oxygen masks dropped.

"Everybody was crying and upset," she said. "You had a few passengers that were very strong, and they kept yelling to people, you know, 'It's OK! We're going to do this!'"

Another passenger, Marty Martinez, posted a brief Facebook Live video showing him donning his oxygen mask. "Something is wrong with our plane!" he wrote. "It appears we are going down! Emergency landing! Southwest flight from NYC to Dallas!"

Southwest said the Boeing 737-700 left New York's LaGuardia Airport shortly after 10:30 a.m. ET, bound for Dallas Love Field. The airport said the plane had landed "safely" and that passengers were being brought into the terminal.

资料来源：https://www.usatoday.com/story/news/nation/2018/04/17/southwest-flight-makes-emergency-landing-philadelphia/524503002/

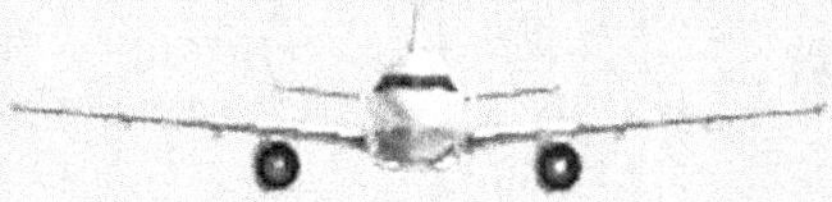

Unit Thirteen Maintenance and Servicing

Text

Passage

Aircraft maintenance is the overhaul, repair, inspection or modification of an aircraft or aircraft components. As an indispensable segment of aviation industry, it plays a crucial role in maintaining the good performance of an aircraft, improving its usability and ensuring flight safety. It is the most important pre-flight activity.

Aircraft maintenance and servicing possibly began with human's first attempt to fly with the airplane which was still a big wooden-structured fabric-covered machine. These wooden machines can easily get wrecked during repair due to the fragile structure. As time went by, great technical advances promoted the evolution of a more sophisticated repair system to cope with those complicated-designed airplanes. The maintenance tasks, personnel and inspection procedures are all tightly regulated. Professional maintenance engineers are trained who must be licensed by local aviation authority before they overhaul the airframe, engines and systems.

Manufacturers are responsible for the satisfactory maintenance of any devices of the aircraft. They must get a Certificate of Airworthiness granted by relevant authorities in order to assure their potential customers of the safety of a new aircraft. They have to compile maintenance manuals and Service Bulletins stating the maintenance and servicing of the aircraft and its components and continually update these data based on the feedback of the pilots who drive the aircraft.

The periods during which each part of an aircraft must be inspected, the type and degree of the inspection, and the replacement of certain components based on flying hours, numbers of landing and other criterias are all stipulated in the maintenance schedule which the airline operator must submit to the airworthiness authority in order to maintain his fleet.To get the approval, some basic requirements must be satisfied, including the provision of suitable hangars and workshops, necessary tools and facilities, quality and reliability control, complete training system and equipment and so on.

The hangers should be big enough to hold a wide-bodied airplane. In a typical hanger, huge stagings, equipped with multi-storey working platforms, lighting, lifts and conveyors, are installed around the aircraft so that each part can be thoroughly checked or repaired by the maintenance personnel.

Maintenance requirements vary for different types of aircraft. And the time-intervals for the maintenance of each part of the aircraft are also different. For instance, engines receive regular inspection at about 500 flying-hour intervals, and the cabin windows and other openings in the fuselage need inspecting about every 300 flying hours. Generally speaking, aircraft undergo light checks at 50-60 flying hours, overnight checks at 300-600 hours and full overhaul every 3,600 flying hours.

New words

1. overhaul [əʊvə'hɔ:l]	v. 彻底检修，翻修
2. modification [ˌmɒdɪfɪ'keɪʃ(ə)n]	n. 修改，改变，改造
3. indispensable [ɪndɪ'spensəb(ə)l]	adj. 不可缺少的；绝对必要的；责无旁贷的
4. usability [ˌju:zə'bɪliti]	n. 可用性；合用
5. fabric ['fæbrɪk]	n. 棉（亚麻，丝，毛）织品；面料；布料
6. wreck [rek]	v./n. 失事；遭难；损坏
7. fragile ['frædʒaɪl]	adj. 易碎的；脆的
8. sophisticated [sə'fɪstɪkeɪtɪd]	adj. 复杂的；精细的；富有经验的
9. airframe ['eəfreɪm]	n. 机身
10. compile [kəm'paɪl]	v. 编译；编制；编辑
11. stipulate ['stɪpjʊleɪt]	v. 规定；保证；规制
12. hangar ['hæŋə]	n. 飞机库；飞机棚
13. staging ['steɪdʒɪŋ]	n. 分段运输；脚手架
	v. 表演；展现；分阶段进行
14. multi-storey ['mʌltiˌstɔ:ri]	adj. 多层的；有多层楼的
15. conveyor [kən'veɪə]	n. 运输机；传送带；传播者
16. interval ['ɪntəv(ə)l]	n. 间隔；区间
17. fuselage ['fju:zəlɑ:ʒ]	n. 飞机机身；机身阻力

Phrases and expressions

1. maintenance and servicing	机身维护与保养
2. aircraft component	飞机构成
3. Certificate of Airworthiness	试航证
4. maintenance manual	维修手册
5. Service Bulletin	服务通告
6. working platform	工作平台

Notes

1. Aircraft maintenance and servicing possibly began with human's first attempt to fly with the airplane which was still a big wooden-structured fabric-covered machine.

在人类首次尝试飞机飞行时可能就已经有了飞机维护与维修。当时的飞机还只是由棉质物覆盖的木质结构的机器。

2. The periods during which each part of an aircraft must be inspected, the type and degree of the inspection, and the replacement of certain components based on flying hours, numbers of landing and other criterias are all stipulated in the maintenance schedule which the airline operator must submit to the airworthiness authority in order to maintain his fleet.

维修日程规定了飞机每一部分要接受检查的时间，检查的类型和程度以及依据飞行小时数、着陆次数和其他标准而对某些零部件进行的更换。航空公司须将这些资料呈递给适航当局以便维持其维修团队。

3. In a typical hanger, huge stagings, equipped with multi-storey working platforms, lighting, lifts and conveyors, are installed around the aircraft so that each part can be thoroughly checked or repaired by the maintenance personnel.

在机库里，飞机周围建造了巨大的检修架，上面配备了多层工作平台、灯光设施、升降机和传送带，这样机务维修人员便可以对飞机每一部分进行彻底详细的检查和修理。

Exercises

I. Translate the following words or phrases into English.

1. 增压系统
2. 空调系统
3. 液压系统
4. 电气系统
5. 通信系统
6. 飞行操纵系统
7. 防火系统
8. 防冰系统
9. 飞机状态监控系统
10. 自动数据交换系统

II. Read and translate the following short passages into Chinese or English.

1. Today, several aviation-related career fields are suffering workforce shortages ever great number of workers will be needed in the future. Experts at Boeing and Airbus forecast a labor shortage in the aviation industry and predict a need of up to 600,000 aircraft maintenance technicians by 2031. In recent years, heavy maintenance, also known as Maintenance, Repair and Overhaul (MRO) activities, were outsourced to foreign companies to save costs. Yet, despite the forecasted labor needs, market growth and fair compensation, few women still appear to enter or stay in the aircraft maintenance career field.

2. Many maintenance tasks, especially in heavy maintenance, may not be completed in a single shift. Aircraft maintenance technicians often take work in progress by colleagues, and

spend the incomplete work for a change of team. The need for accuracy and efficiency of information transfer in many cases, without having time to have a meeting to pass the service is a crucial aspect of maintenance work. Although a shift change create challenges for communication, they also offer opportunities to detect and correct errors, where the task of delivery is an opportunity to identify the problem and fix it.

3. 机务维修手册是非常重要的文件，保证了飞机维修工作的顺利开展。其里面包含了很多重要内容，使得飞机具有持续的适航性。然而，传统手册里大量的文字内容以及静止的图片已经无法准确完美地呈现飞机复杂精密的结构以及维修流程。为了提高手册的准确性以及描述力，人们已经研发了一种新型的 3D 飞机维修手册。

4. D 检，有时也被称作大修检查，是到目前为止最全面、要求最高的飞机检查。一架飞机每六到十年经历一次 D 检。这种检查几乎会将整架飞机拆开进行检查和修理。甚至机身蒙皮上的漆也会完全去除以便进行深入检查。完成这种检查通常花费 50 000 工时和两个月的时间。这主要取决于飞机本身情况以及参与的技术人员的数量。平均每架商业飞机在退役前会经历 3 次 D 检。

III. Answer the following questions based on the text.

1. How do you understand aircraft maintenance and servicing?
2. Who compile the maintenance manuals and Service Bulletins? What are they used for?
3. What does maintenance schedule include?
4. What does a typical hanger like?
5. How long does an airliner need to be inspected?

Supplementary Reading Material

The Importance of Aircraft Maintenance and Service

All aircrafts, big and small, must be serviced regularly, according to the specifications provided by the manufacturer. But there are different types of service and maintenance checks, and also different ways that service is scheduled.

Additionally, all planes should be regularly inspected before each flight.

While individual manufacturer requirements do differ, light planes generally need an annual inspection to check the condition of the plane, as well as service maintenance after a specified number of flying hours.

Service and Maintenance Checks

It should be obvious, but the more you fly your plane, the more frequently you will need to have it serviced. This is why manufacturers commonly specify flight hours rather than timeframes for service and maintenance checks. So, for instance, an annual condition check carried out to ensure that the plane conforms to the airworthiness "type" certificate issued when it was originally inspected after manufacture might be required more frequently (perhaps every 100 hours) if the plane is used often, or for commercial purposes. For this check, all access plates are normally removed, and everything that can possibly be checked, is checked, including retractable landing gear and related mechanisms, as well as engine compression.

More frequent maintenance service checks would include checking of critical bolts including those that connect the propeller to the engine, as well as replacement of engine oil. Oil changes could be required as frequently as every 25 hours flying time.

Aircraft tires, like those used for automobiles, must be replaced when the rubber tread begins to wear. Generally this will be determined by the friction caused between the tires and airfield surface, which in turn will be directly affected by the number of landings made in the plane.

Visual Aircraft Inspections

All light aircrafts should be inspected visually before each flight. Typically the pilot or co-pilot will check fuel levels, engine oil level, cable connections and internal parts, and generally look out for any damage that might have occurred. It is always good to check the area below where the plane has been parked to make sure there isn't evidence of leaking fluids.

Federal Aviation Administration (FAA) Requirements for Airworthiness

While FAA maintenance checks are more stringent for airlines carrying passengers, as well as commercial planes, and military aircrafts, the types of checks followed provide additional insight into how often aircraft should be serviced. These do not preclude the checks and inspections required by the manufacturer. FAA checks are commonly referred to as A, B, C and D checks, D being the most comprehensive.

A checks are done after 125 flight hours, depending on the type of aircraft and aircraft cycle of takeoff and landing, and take between 20 and 50 man hours to complete. A checks on airliners are usually performed at the airport gate, overnight.

B checks are performed, on average, every six months. They take between 120 and 150 man hours to complete, and are usually executed in the aircraft hangar.

C checks are commonly performed every two years, or according to the flight hours defined by the manufacturer of the aircraft. This is an extensive check and involves the inspection of most of the aircraft components. It can take one to two weeks to complete, and as many as 6,000 man hours. These checks are generally performed in hangars located at a dedicated maintenance base.

D checks are comprehensive and sometimes refers to as a "heavy maintenance visit." They are done every six years or so and involve thorough inspection and a complete overhaul. They can take as many as 50,000 man-hours over a period of two months to complete. Because these checks are so expensive, many airlines prefer to phase their craft out instead.

Where to Go to Service Your Aircraft or Buy Parts

While many service centers specialize in maintaining specific types of aircraft, there are also companies that specialize in the repair, supply and overhaul of a wider range of fixed-wing planes. Some, like Prime Industries, also supply quality parts and components for a wide range of rotary and fixed-wing aircraft.

资料来源：https://primeindustriesusa.com/aircraft-service/

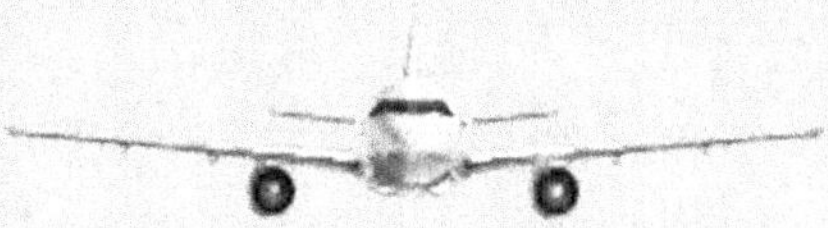

Unit Fourteen

Airports

Text

Passage

The world's large airports are designed as cities with complete facilities. They are exchange points of air transportation and all kinds of ground transportations, serving the demands of travelers, personnel, greeters and those who come to experience and enjoy modern air transport. Because of their close proximity, they are also closely related to the neighborhood.

The earliest aircraft take off and landing sites were grassy fields. The plane could approach at any angle that provided a favorable wind direction. A slight improvement was the dirt-only field, which eliminated the drag from grass. However, these only functioned well in dry conditions. Later, concrete surfaces would allow landings regardless of meteorological conditions.

Aircraft noise is a major cause of noise disturbance to residents living near airports. Sleep can be affected if the airports operate night and early morning flights. Aircraft noise not only occurs from take off and landings, but also ground operations including maintenance and testing of aircraft. Noise has other health effects. Other noise and environmental problems include noise and pollution caused by vehicles on roads leading to the airport. The construction of new airports or addition of runways to existing airports, is often resisted by local residents because of the effect on countryside, historical sites, local flora and fauna. Due to the risk of collision between birds and aircraft, large airports undertake population control programs where they frighten or shoot birds. The construction of airports has been known to change local weather patterns. For example, because they often flatten out large areas, they can be susceptible to fog in areas where fog rarely forms. In addition, they generally replace trees and grass with pavement, they often change drainage patterns in agricultural areas, leading to more flooding, run-off and erosion in the surrounding land. With the progress of science and technology, the construction of the airport has become a double-edged sword.

Fortunately, the construction of the airport is developing in a better direction. The design and manufacture of the aircraft evolves in a larger-size and less-noisy direction. Meanwhile, the increased size of aircraft also reduces the growth rate of the aircraft's take-off and landing times. With their expanding role as centers of trade, travel and employment, the large airports are steadily transforming into good neighbors of the local residential area.

The modern airport must be in harmony with the local residents as far as possible, while taking care of the interests of air passengers, airlines and their own staff. Safe, convenient and normal flights are the three elements that the authorities must consider when they plan and operate airports. Airports must be located in places where there is no obstacle or danger in the approaching and take off lanes, where runways have the proper width and length, equipped with appropriate lighting and necessary radio and radar equipment, and where the taxiway is wide enough to reach a broad apron near the terminal.

In the past many years, airport construction has been focusing on building longer and stronger runways to meet the needs of larger and faster aircraft. However, modern technology is starting to work on shortening the distance. In the distant future, a 12,000-foot runway may be enough for the heaviest and fastest supersonic jet aircraft up to 500 tons loaded weight, even on a hot day when engine power is reduced. The only exceptions are high-altitude airports, where it is necessary to greatly increase the safe distance between take off and landing because of the thin air.

With more and more people using airports, the authorities have made every effort to meet demands of comfort and convenience. They try to shorten the walking distance from arrival point to airplane as possible as they can. They aim to guarantee the best possible access to and from the airport, not only by road and railway, but also by subway and helicopter. They provide sufficient car parking space, construct distinctly signposted and well-equipped terminal buildings. Although few airports are able to fully achieve these requirements, everyone is trying to realize this goal in the smooth process of modernization and expansion.

Most airport names include the location. Many airport names honor a public figure, commonly a politician (e.g. Charles de Gaulle Airport), a monarch like in Chhatrapati Shivaji International Airport, a cultural leader such as in Liverpool John Lennon Airport or a prominent figure in aviation history of the region (e.g. Sydney Kingsford Smith Airport), sometimes even famous poets (e.g. Allama Iqbal International Airport). Some airports have unofficial names, possibly so widely circulated that its official name is little used or even known. Some airport names include the word "International" to indicate their ability to handle international air traffic. This includes some airports that do not have scheduled international airline services (e.g. Albany International Airport).

New words

1. proximity [prɒk'sɪmɪti] n. 亲近；接近，邻近
2. eliminate [ɪ'lɪmɪneɪt] vt. 淘汰；排除，消除；除掉
3. drag [dræg] n. 阻力；拖
4. meteorological [ˌmiːtɪərə'lɒdʒɪkəl] adj. 气象的；气象学的
5. maintenance ['meɪntənəns] n. 维护；维修
6. flora ['flɔrə] n. 植物群；植物区系
7. fauna ['fɔːnə] n. 动物群
8. collision [kə'lɪʒən] n. 碰撞；冲突

9. susceptible [sə'septɪb|ə|l] adj. 易受影响的
10. pavement ['peɪvm(ə)nt] n. 硬路面；人行道
11. drainage ['dreɪnɪdʒ] n. 排水系统
12. obstacle ['ɒbstək|ə|l] n. 障碍物，干扰
13. taxiway ['tæksiweɪ] n.（飞机的）滑行道
14. high-altitude ['haɪ'æltɪtju:d] adj. 高空的
15. monarch ['mɒnək] n. 君主，帝王

Phrases and expressions

1. regardless of 不管，不顾
2. concrete surface 混凝土地面
3. noise disturbance 噪声干扰
4. local resident 当地居民
5. historical site 历史古迹
6. weather pattern 天气模式
7. double-edged sword 双刃剑
8. loaded weight 装载重量
9. terminal building 候机楼
10. public figure 公众人物；社会名人

Notes

1. In the distant future, a 12 000-foot runway may be enough for the heaviest and fastest supersonic jet aircraft up to 500 tons loaded weight, even on a hot day when engine power is reduced.

在遥远的将来，一条12,000英尺长的跑道对于载重多达500吨的最重型和最快超音速喷气机来说是足够的，即使在发动机功率减少的炎热天气里也是如此。

2. Many airport names honor a public figure, commonly a politician (e.g. Charles de Gaulle Airport), a monarch like in Chhatrapati Shivaji International Airport, a cultural leader such as in Liverpool John Lennon Airport or a prominent figure in aviation history of the region (e.g. Sydney Kingsford Smith Airport), sometimes even famous poets (e.g. Allama Iqbal International Airport).

许多机场的名字是以公众人物的名字命名的，这些人物通常是政治家（例如法国巴黎的戴高乐机场）、君王（例如印度孟买的加特拉帕蒂·希瓦吉国际机场）、文化领袖（如英国利物浦的约翰·列侬机场）、航空史上的杰出人物（如澳大利亚悉尼的金斯福德·史密斯机场），有时甚至是著名的诗人（如巴基斯坦拉合尔的阿拉马·伊克巴勒国际机场）。

Exercises

I. The following is the sample infrastructure of a typical airport. Larger airports usually contain more runways and terminals. Learn the name of each part by heart.

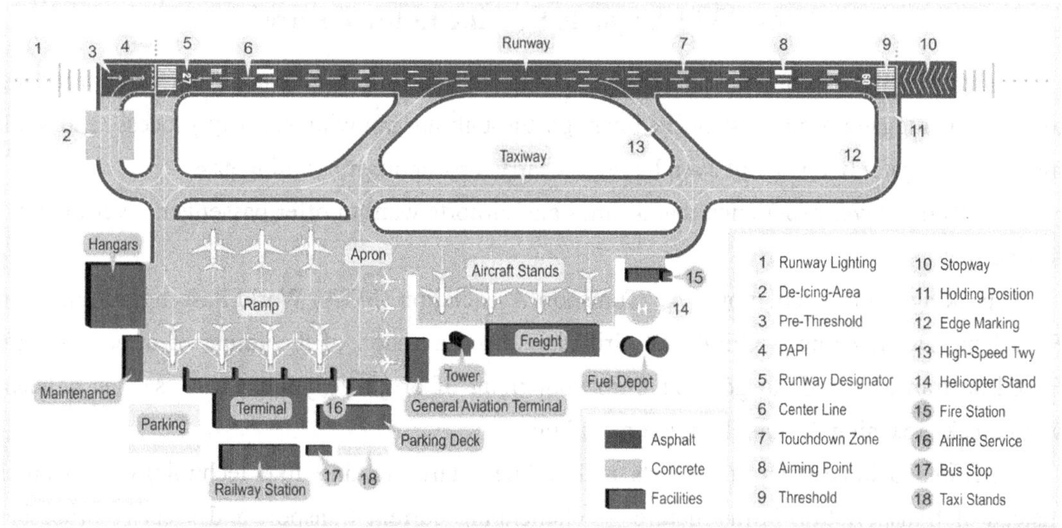

II. Analyze the following sentences grammatically.

1. Due to the risk of collision between birds and aircraft, large airports undertake population control programs where they frighten or shoot birds.

2. The construction of new airports or addition of runways to existing airports, is often resisted by local residents because of the effect on countryside, historical sites, local flora and fauna.

3. The modern airport must be in harmony with the local residents as far as possible, while taking care of the interests of air passengers, airlines and their own staff. Safe, convenient and normal flights are the three elements that the authorities must consider when they plan and operate airports.

III. Answer the following questions based on the text.

1. Where does the earliest aircraft take off and land?

2. Why is the construction of new airports or addition of runways to existing airports often resisted by local residents?

3. How does the construction of airport change local weather patterns?

4. What are the three elements that the authorities must consider when they plan and operate airports?

Supplementary Reading Material

What Will Airports Be Like in the Future?

Imagine getting from your home to your plane to your hotel and back again without having to lug your luggage around, stand in lines, go through an annoying security process, and walk miles to your gate. Imagine not even having to carry a passport or boarding pass.

That's the travel experience that airlines and airports want to offer passengers over the next few decades.

Speaking at the International Air Transport Association (IATA) World Passenger Summit in Barcelona, Dubai Airports CEO Paul Griffiths shared a vision of the future of airport design. Based on transport pods to get you from your point of origin to your concourse, the concept would make reaching the gate less of a marathon.

Griffiths believes that if airports and airlines start thinking like technology companies instead of transportation infrastructure — challenging current transport and security processes and terminal design — that we can enjoy a much improved air travel experience.

"We need to take a leaf out of the books of Uber, Amazon, Facebook and eBay and all of those who have applied technology and process design to re-imagine their entire business around customer convenience," he said. "This would trigger a dramatic redesign of airports."

Biometric ID and Security

In the future, airlines and airports want to get rid of check-in desks and security lines. Instead, passengers may get their luggage picked up at home or at the hotel, and delivered again to their residence at the destination.

Passengers' identities could be confirmed using biometric screening without having to present security documents, and advanced screening technology would ensure passengers are safe without having to stop to scan bags, laptops and shampoo bottles, or remove shoes and belts.

"Imagine an airport with no check-in, no immigration, and discreet non-intrusive security all enabled by a single identity database securely held in the cloud and available to those who currently need physical evidence of our identity as we travel," Griffiths said. "The possibility then re-emerges to reorder the entire travel process around the customer's service, rather than around the convenience of everyone else."

Sound unreal? Much of the technology needed to deliver this experience is already in place.

Biometric identity is gaining momentum in the aviation industry, with plans to go beyond today's facial or fingerprint scanners, to having passengers simply walk by and be recognized with a combination of biometric "footprints". It's a concept right out of science-fiction films, but it could be deployed within the next five to 10 years.

"The question is can we get it over the line with the various governmental departments who hold the key to this," Griffiths said.

Pods to Planes

With baggage taken care of and security lines eliminated, Griffiths says, airports can be designed based on smaller concourse nodes, where passengers can find their gates and lounges, perhaps some retail and dining.

They would be transported directly and quickly on pod-like public transport, which could be using a pod-concept, like Hyperloop, or something simpler, like "platooned" trains in which cars can split off to go to multiple destinations.

"Pods will be able to take customers from their chosen point of entry directly to their plane in a matter of a few minutes without leaving their seat," Griffiths said.

Turning Giant Terminals into Light Boxes

Griffiths explained to T+L how he imagines this future airport experience might work.

"You could have a platform at a curb — people could arrive on their cars on a bus or another train — and just walk along the curb," he said. "You could have all sorts of machinery able to take the baggage from them, and they could board a specific pod that is heading to connect them to their flight — to Vancouver, or Delhi, or Bangkok."

"They could get in that pod and the whole system could leave the station at the same time. Then, the pods split off to the individual concourses from which they have a very short walk to their aircraft," he said. "You can actually have very convenient locations, multiple locations over a city, at which people could enter this transit system.

"So you don't need car parks. You don't need a terminal. You don't need all of these massive baggage systems."

Dubai is already working on these plans for the future of air transport, with the more manageable concourse Light Box plans for the future of Dubai World Central airport. This airport redesign would complement the new city-planning vision for Dubai World Central which would include the types of ground transport and biometric advancements Griffiths talks about, to be introduced over time.

Griffiths says that the concourse node concept is mainly intended for airports which have not yet been built, though a number of these features for biometric identity, baggage collection, and even more efficient ground transport could be fitted into existing airports in one form or another.

"I'm not suggesting that you could go the whole hog with every single airport," he said, "but what I'm suggesting is that these mass transit and distribution systems could be retrofitted into existing airport environments, depending on the geography of each airport."

But what about the airports that won't be retrofitted?

"I'm sure that it's possible to use them for alternative uses," Griffiths said. "Maybe art displays."

资料来源：http://www.travelandleisure.com/airlines-airports/building-airport-of-the-future

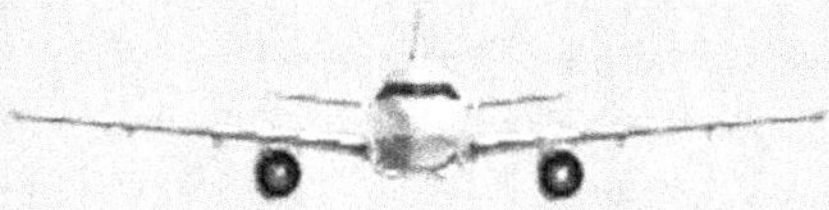

Unit Fifteen

Airport Fire Services

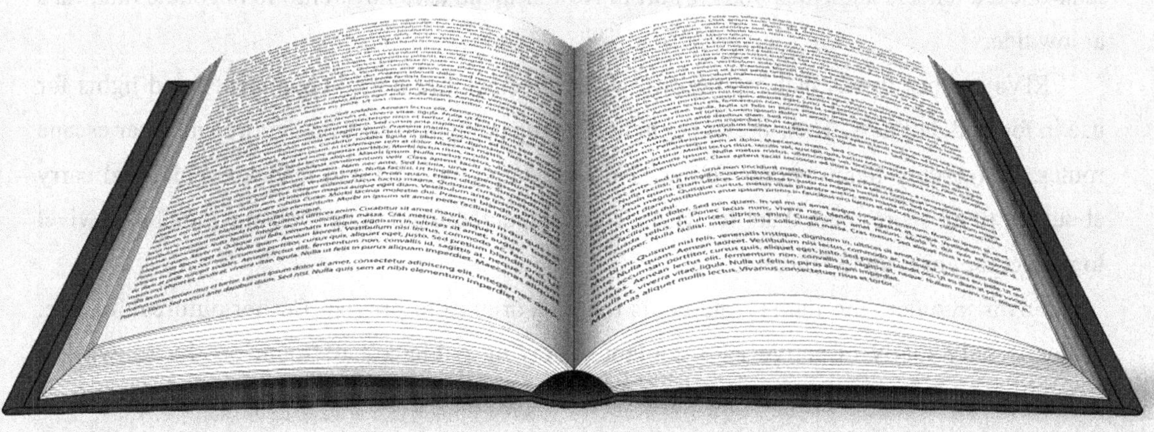

Text

Passage

Seventy-five percent of all aircraft accidents occur within half a mile of an airport. Aircraft fires are rare-London's Heathrow Airport had two in 1977-but an airport is not permitted to operate without an efficient fire service.

Airport fire services will turn out on full emergency stand-by on the slightest indication that something is wrong with a landing plane: a deflated tyre, a circuit-breaker out in any important system, a warning light in the flight deck. They turn out on average once a day at a major airport, and are always on stand-by in bad weather or fog. During an emergency the fire service provides general emergency help, carrying stretchers and aiding disabled people.

Aircraft burn quickly, giving fire fighters under three minutes to reach them and carry out control and rescue operations. Until the 1960s, airport fire-fighting equipment consisted of little more than modified versions of that used by municipal fire services. Now every major airport is equipped with rapid intervention vehicles (RIVs) able to reach the runways within two minutes of an alarm. Heavy duty vehicles are designed to cross rough ground to reach a distant runway (by a circuitous route, they cannot drive across runways in use) or the overshoot and undershoot areas where most fatalities occur.

No airport is awarded a licence unless it conforms to national standards based on ICAO recommendations, but each airport is equipped with its own needs. Some Indian airports have tank-tracked tenders and Auckland Airport in New Zealand uses hovercraft to negotiate mud flats at low tide.

RIVs are fast trucks that carry foam, water, medical and rescue equipments, and lights for use in fog and darkness. Their crews begin holding operations to contain the fire and clear escape routes. Heavy-duty foam tenders follow. They are large, but fast and manoeuvrable, and carry about ten times more foam than the RIVs. Turret-mounted foam guns ("blabbermouths") swivel to project the foam up to 300 feet.

Foam smothers the flames and cools the area around to prevent further outbreak of fire. Water is only really effective as a coolant. Spraying a blanket of foam on the runway to prevent a malfunctioning plane from catching fire on landing is now thought to be a waste of time, but foam is useful for fires that break out during refuelling when a build-up of static electricity in the tank sparks the fuel. Kerosene is less inflammable than the fuels used by many airlines, but more expensive.

Powder is more effective on localized fire in wheels or tyres, or in electrical apparatus, but it produces toxic fumes on contact with foam. Inert-vaporizing gases, such as Halon 1200, attack oxygen and are particularly useful for engine fires.

The emergency services are stationed at various points around the airfield, and are in radio contact with each other, the central station and the control tower.

Airport fire-fighters wear flame-resistant aluminized clothing and are equipped with breathing apparatus against smoke and the toxic fumes produced by burning aircraft furnishings. They train daily, and practise their craft on old fuselages in remote parts of the airfield.

New words

1. deflate [di'fleit] v. 使泄气，使瘪下去，使缩小；排气
2. circuit ['sɜːkit] n. 电路，线路；环道
3. breaker ['breikə] n. 电流断路器
4. stretcher ['stretʃə] n. 担架；脚踏板；延伸器
5. disable [dis'eib|ə|l] v. 使无能；使伤残；使无资格
6. rescue ['reskjuː] v. 援救，营救
   n. 援救，营救
7. modify ['mɒdifai] v. 修造，更改
8. version ['vɜːʃ(ə)n] n. 形式；版本；译本
9. municipal [mju(ː)'nisip(ə)l] adj. 市的；市政的；地方自治的
10. overshoot [əuvə'ʃuːt] n. 目测高；着陆时越过指定地点
11. undershoot [ʌndə'ʃuːt] n. 目测低；着陆时未达跑道
12. fatality [fə'tæliti] n. 灾难；死亡（事故）；宿命
13. recommendation [ˌrekəmen'deiʃ(ə)n] n. 推荐；建议；推荐信
14. tender ['tendə] n. 供应船；补给船；小船；（机场的）地面保障车辆
15. Auckland ['ɔːklənd] n. 奥克兰（新西兰北岛首府）
16. hovercraft ['hɔvəkrɑːft] n. 气垫船；气垫车
17. foam [fəum] n. 泡沫；泡沫材料；灭火泡沫
18. manoeuvrable [mə'nuvərəbl] adj. 操纵灵敏的；机动的；可调动的
19. turret ['tʌrit] n. 六角转台；回转装置；旋转架
20. blabbermouth ['blæbəmauθ] n. 喋喋不休的人；长舌者
21. swivel ['swivl] v. 旋转
22. smother ['smʌðə] v. 闷熄；闷火；使窒息；抑制
23. coolant ['kuːl(ə)nt] n. 冷却剂

24. malfunction ['mæl'fʌŋkʃən] n. 失灵；发生故障
25. static ['stætik] adj. 静的；静态的
26. apparatus [ˌæpə'reitəs] n. 设备；装置；仪器；器官
27. vaporize ['veipəraiz] v. 使蒸发；使汽化
28. aluminise [ə'lju:minaiz] v. 镀（涂敷、渗）铝化

Phrases and expressions

1. airport fire service 机场消防队
2. deflated tyre 瘪气的轮胎
3. circuit-breaker 电路自动保险电门
4. fire fighter 消防员
5. fire-fighter equipment 消防设备
6. circuitous route 迂回路线
7. runway-in-use 使用跑道
8. overshoot area 目测过高地区
9. undershoot area 目测低接地区
10. tank-tracked tender 坦克履带补给车
11. heavy-duty foam tender 重型泡沫灭火器消防车
12. turret-duty foam tender 装在旋转架上的泡沫灭火枪
13. electrical apparatus 电气设备

Abbreviation

RIV rapid intervention vehicle 快速介入车

Notes

1. London's Heathrow Airport had two in 1977 ...
伦敦希思罗机场 1977 年发生两起（飞机着火事件）……

2. ... the overshoot and undershoot areas where most fatalities occur
最容易发生事故的目测高接和低接地区

3. Spraying a blanket of foam on the runway to prevent a malfunctioning plane from catching fire on landing is now thought to be a waste of time, ...
在跑道上撒上一层泡沫以防止带故障的飞机在着陆时起火，现在看来是浪费时间。

Exercises

I. Read and translate the following passages into Chinese.

1. The rapid intervention fire/rescue vehicle is designed to accelerate to 70 mph as fast as a

sports car, despite the weight of foam and equipment carried. It carries 200 gals (240 US gals) of a concentrated, ready-mixed water and foam solution, first aid and rescue equipment which is used to contain the fire and keep aircraft escape routes open until the main fire-fighting force arrives. This six-wheeled model carries an aluminium ladder. The versatile chassis can be fitted with stretchers and other special equipment, for use as an ambulance.

2. The heavy-duty fire tender can discharge 9,000 gals (10,800 US gals) of water or foam a minute through its monitor, and 900 gals (1,080 US gals) through each of its two handlines, while moving forward or backward.

3. The heavy-duty airfield crash truck can be operated by one man, or carry a crew of five. It holds over 3,000 gals of water and over 360 gals of foam, and travels at 60 mph. It throws a 300 ft jet.

4. Search and rescue is a service which seeks missing aircraft and assists those found to be in need of assistance.

II. Analyse the following sentences grammatically.

1. During an emergency the fire service provides general emergency help, carrying stretchers and aiding disabled people.

2. Aircraft burn quickly, giving fire fighters under three minutes to reach them and carry out control and rescue operations.

3. No airport is awarded a licence unless it conforms to national standards based on ICAO recommendations, but each airport is equipped according to its own needs.

4. Foam is useful for fires that break out during refuelling when a build-up of static electricity in the tank sparks the fuel.

5. Kerosene is less inflammable than the fuels used by many airlines, but more expensive.

III. Answer the following questions based on the text.

1. When will airport fire services turn out on full emergency stand-by?

2. How long are RIVs able to reach the runways? What do RIVs carry?

3. What do heavy-duty foam tenders carry? Are there any guns mounted on the tenders?

4. Is kerosene cheaper than the fuels used by many airlines?

5. What do fire-fighters wear and are equipped with?

Supplementary Reading Material

Behind the Scenes with an Airport Firefighter

Firefighting is the hottest job at an airport so here at your Heathrow we've gone behind the scenes with Airport Fire Manager Gary Barthram.

Joining the Airport Fire Service in 1988 for London City Airport as a fire fighter, Gary moved to Stansted in 1990 before transferring to Heathrow Airport in 1995 and moving up the ranks to Airport Fire Manager. He describes his job as "an ideal match with great diversity in a really dynamic and interesting location".

What's your favourite part of the job?

The diversity, every day is different. When I arrive on shift, I never know what my day is going to throw at me. Being able to serve the airport community when there is an emergency or an incident is something I love. I know if a serious situation goes as we plan, lives can be saved. In my present role as Airport Fire Manager I take on the role of Silver Commander on the incident site for the Airport Fire Service.

What equipment do you use for training?

We use a mock-up of a 747/MD11 aircraft made of steel to re-enact fire scenarios. The mock-up aircraft has internal and external parts such as the fuselage, undercarriage and an engine along with beds, seats and compartments. It also has the ability to be filled with cosmetic smoke to allow crews to train for search and rescue operations when visibility is virtually nil.

As we also attend domestic fire calls, road traffic collisions and serious medical calls within the airport boundary, we have a drill tower and use old vehicles to practice casualty extrications. The police provide us with a selection of cars every few months so we can cut them up, remove the roofs and doors in practice scenarios.

An exciting day on the job may not be the best way to describe it. But what gets the adrenalin pumping for you and your team?

Firefighters by nature enjoy attending incidents and helping people, that's why they join. Even though our adrenalin may be pumping attending an incident, we have to be prepared for the fact that there could be a devastating outcome for another person. We also have to be very careful when using the word "exciting", as an integral part of the job is remaining calm at incidents that often provoke all sorts of emotion. A successful day for me would be to attend an incident, deal with it effectively so that no one is hurt and provide a good professional service to both internal and external stakeholders.

What would an average day include?

We don't really have an average day. We attend to all sorts of incidents. We attend to anything that is life-threating at the airport or on the roads around it; this could include a heart attack air or land-side, a drug mule incident where a passenger has transported drugs within their body and has ended up in a serious condition, or a car crash that we have to cut a victim out of.

We all have set duties to do every day and night including practical and theoretical training, testing and inspections, and cleaning of vehicles and equipment. The crews have to keep physically fit so we give them time for physical training and provide facilities to do this. Obviously if we get an emergency call then everything is put on hold until the emergency is dealt with.

How soon can a crew respond to a fire?

We have a maximum of three minutes from time of call to time of attendance. The Airport Fire Service is different to the Local Authority Fire Service as we have much tighter response times set by the Civil Aviation Authority. The requirement is due to aircraft on the airfield, the size of the aircraft, and the large amount of passengers and fuel involved. Once in attendance, all of the crews are trained to assess the situation in front of them and act dynamically without the need for orders in the early stages of an incident.

Interesting stats?

- In 2012 we attended 1018 calls consisting of aircraft, domestic, medical and special service incidents.
- There are four watches under the Airport Fire Manager's command, consisting of 27 personnel on each watch. The teams do 12 hour shifts, averaging 42 hours a week and covering the 24/7 operation.
- Our Major Foam Tenders can produce 5,600 L of water and foam per minute and hold 11,200 L of water. We have just taken possession of a new fleet of 8 Foam Tenders with the latest technology to enhance our operation on the airfield.
- We have a 42 m aerial ladder platform — the highest in the country. We need this to reach to the top deck of an A380.

资料来源：http://your.heathrow.com/behind-the-scenes-with-an-airport-firefighter/

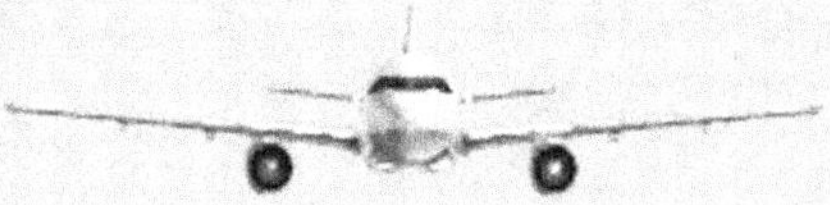

Unit Sixteen
Airport Security

Text

Passage

Each day a considerable number of people travel by air from all over the world. And the high concentration of people at the airports makes these places a potential target for smuggling, theft, illegal immigration, terrorism and other kinds of crimes. The cargo terminals isolated from the main airport buildings are also frequented by thieves and pilferers especially during goods loading or delivery, which has caused great financial loss each year.

Airport security aims to prevent the occurrence of any threats or potentially dangerous situations, ensuring the safety of the passengers, crew and aircraft and supporting national security and counter-terrorism policy. To safeguard civil aviation against unlawful interference, a series of advanced techniques and methods are employed.

Terrorism is the most terrible threat. Ever since a Peruvian Airlines plane was hijacked in 1930, aerial piracy has never stopped. And half of the over 400 hijack events were successful since 1969. Thus countries throughout the world began to contribute more to improving airport security and flight safety. Especially since the September 11 attacks, security screening has become significantly tightened for both domestic and international flight. Airports and airlines at risk may have air cargo X-rayed or as at the Lufthansa terminals, containerized cargo will be decompressed for 12 hours to avoid bomb explosion in cargo holds during flight. Some cargo may have to be stored in a safe place for more than 24 hours or go through some special disposal procedures authorized by aviation authority.

Passengers will also have to undergo a series of security checks since they enter the terminal. They must show their flight ticket, boarding pass, and valid identification, like ID card, passport or certificate of soldiers. Some countries also fingerprint travelers or use Retina and Iris scanning to detect crimes. Besides, scanning facilities including hand-held detectors, metal detectors and full-body scanning machines in which passengers are essentially X-rayed are utilized to check for potential hidden dangerous goods on their persons like explosives, flammable objects, toxic substances, weapons and so on. In some countries, specially trained personnel may engage passengers in a conversation to detect threats rather than solely depending on equipment. Generally people who have finished security check would stay in a secure or sterile area where the exit gates are located. The passengers discharged from airliners could also stay there since they are exempt from recheck if disembarking from a domestic flight. Yet even so, they are still subject to search at any time if necessary.

Because physical searches are undignified, time-consuming and inefficient, most airports screen passengers using electro-magnetic metal-detectors. And the travelers' carry-on items like handbags are usually visually inspected through low-dosage X-ray equipment. At some airports, "sniffer" dogs may also be used to detect those hidden dangerous prohibited goods.

However, airport security relies ultimately on teams of well-trained detection equipment operators as well as experienced security staff.

New words

1. smuggling ['smʌglɪŋ] n. 走私
2. terrorism ['terərɪzəm] n. 恐怖主义，恐怖行动
3. pilferer ['pɪlfərə] n. 小偷
4. safeguard ['seɪfgɑːd] v. 保护，护卫
5. Peruvian [pə'ruːvjən] a. 秘鲁的；秘鲁人的
6. hijack ['haɪdʒæk] v. 抢劫，劫机
7. piracy ['paɪrəsɪ] n. 海盗行为；剽窃；著作权侵害
8. containerize [kən'teɪnəraɪz] v. 用集装箱装；以货柜运送
9. decompress [ˌdiːkəm'pres] v. 使减压，使解除压力
10. disposal [dɪ'spəʊz(ə)l] n. 处理；支配；清理；安排
11. fingerprint ['fɪŋgəprɪnt] n. 指纹；手印
12. retina ['rɛtənə] n. 视网膜
13. iris ['aɪrɪs] n. 虹膜；鸢尾属植物
14. undignified [ʌn'dɪgnɪfaɪd] adj. 不庄重的，不体面的
15. sniffer [snɪfə] n. 嗅探器

Phrases and expressions

1. airport security 机场安检
2. illegal immigration 非法移民；非法入境
3. cargo terminal 货物码头；货物终点站
4. unlawful interference 非法干预
5. cargo hold 货舱
6. security check 安检
7. boarding pass 登机证
8. toxic substance 有毒物质
9. exempt from 免除
10. electro-magnetic metal-detector 电磁金属探测器

Notes

1. Airports and airlines at risk may have air cargo X-rayed or as at the Lufthansa terminals, containerized cargo will be decompressed for 12 hours to avoid bomb explosion in cargo holds during flight.

面临风险的机场和航空公司使用X射线检查货物，或者像汉莎航空公司货运站那样，将集装的货物减压12小时，以避免飞行中货舱发生爆炸。

2. Besides, scanning facilities including hand-held detectors, metal detectors and full-body scanning machines in which passengers are essentially X-rayed are utilized to check for potential hidden dangerous goods on their persons like explosives, flammable objects, toxic substances, weapons and so on.

除此之外，扫描设施还包括手持探测器、金属探测器和全身扫描机器，这种机器实质上对人进行X射线扫描。这些设备用于检测藏匿的随身携带的危险物品，如爆炸物、易燃物、有毒物品、武器等。

3. Generally people who have finished security check would stay in a secure or sterile area where the exit gates are located.

通常，完成安检的乘客可以去候机隔离区等待登机。

Exercises

I. Translate the following words or phrases into English.

1. 海关检查柜台
2. 免税商品
3. 违禁品
4. 机场公安
5. 候机隔离区
6. 安检门
7. 登机口
8. 传送带
9. 易燃物品
10. 易爆物品
11. 腐蚀性物品
12. 放射性物品
13. 有毒物品
14. 液态物品

II. Read and translate the following short passages into Chinese.

1. Explosives trace detectors (ETD) are explosive detection equipment capable of detecting

explosives of small magnitude. The equipment takes s sample of non-visible "trace" amounts of particulates to detect and analyze the contents. Such explosives detectors are highly sensitive, accurate and versatile non-contact screening systems and can be employed in airports and other vulnerable areas considered susceptible to acts of unlawful interference.

2. Dogs' keen sense of smell makes them precious assets in all kinds of security applications. However, their use is sometimes subject to some intrinsic restrictions. This has sparked a drive over the past decade to develop artificial sniffer devices known as "chemical sniffers" or "electronic noses" to complement or even replace sniffer dogs in security checks. Like dogs, these machines can detect residual traces indicating the presence of or recent contact with prohibited substances such as explosives or drugs. Such equipment can be used in various places like borders, airports or other important security checkpoints.

3. Aviation security could be improved with the use of databases containing passenger's personal information, technology such as full body scans and better information-sharing. But the changes would require greater tolerance of intrusions and far more effective government supervision. Travelers probably would have to become accustomed to the feeling that authorities know a lot more about them, their families and their associates, and that they are being looked at by machines in intimate ways that once were unthinkable.

III. Answer the following questions based on the text.

1. Why are there crimes at airports?
2. Do you know any terrorism activities involving air travel?
3. What can airports do to ensure there are no dangerous goods in the air cargo?
4. What do airports usually do to detect the hidden dangerous goods on passengers?
5. What does security depend on?

Supplementary Reading Material

Best Ways to Prepare for Airport Security Screenings

Whether you've flown five times or 500 times, you know that getting through airport security can be an annoying, time-consuming process. By the time you've waited in line, handed over your ID, bundled your possessions into a plastic bin and walked through the metal detector, you're already tired of traveling.

While you can't avoid going through airport security screening, there are things you can do to speed up the screening process.

Pack Properly

Check TSA regulations to see which items belong in checked baggage (knives, for example) and which should be placed in your carry-on. Review your airline's policies, too, in case checked baggage fees and rules have changed since you last traveled. Leave prohibited items at home. Never put expensive items like cameras or jewelry into your checked baggage. Carry all of your prescription drugs with you.

Organize Tickets and Travel Documents

Remember to bring a government-issued photo ID, such as a driver's license, passport or military ID card, to the airport. Your ID must show your name, date of birth, gender and an expiration date. Place your tickets and ID in a spot that's easy to reach so you won't have to fumble around for them in the security line. (Tip: Bring a passport for all international flights.)

Prepare Your Carry-On Items

In the US, you may bring one carry-on bag and one personal item – typically a laptop, purse or briefcase – into the passenger compartment on most airlines.

Discount airlines, such as Spirit, have stricter rules. Be sure to remove all sharp items, such as knives, multitools and scissors, from your carry-on luggage. Place all liquid, gel and aerosol items into one quart-sized, clear plastic bag with a zip-top closure. No single item in this bag may contain more than 3.4 ounces (100 milliliters) of aerosol, gel or liquid.

Partially-used larger containers will not pass the security screening; leave them at home. While you may bring unlimited quantities of powdered substances onto the plane, TSA screeners may perform extra tests on any powder you carry aboard.

Pack Your Medications

Medications are not subject to the 3.4 ounces / 100-milliliter limit, but you must tell the TSA screeners that you have drugs with you and present them for inspection. It's easier to do this if you pack your medications together. If you use an insulin pump or another medical device, you'll need to declare that at the checkpoint, too. Place all of your medications in your carry-on bag. Never carry medications in your checked bag.

Prep Your Laptop

When you reach the metal detector, you'll be asked to take your laptop computer out of its bag and place it into a separate plastic bin, unless you carry it in a special "checkpoint friendly" bag. This bag cannot contain anything except your laptop.

Ban the Bling

While dressing up to travel is perfectly acceptable, almost any large metal object will set off the detector. Pack your belts with large buckles, glitzy bangle bracelets and extra change in your carry-on bag; don't wear or carry them on your person.

Dress for Success

If you have body piercings, consider removing your jewelry before you start the airport screening process. Wear slip-on shoes so that you can easily remove them. (Wear socks, too, if the idea of walking barefoot on the airport's floor bothers you.) Be prepared to undergo a pat-down screening if your clothing is very loose-fitting or if you wear a head covering that could conceal a weapon. (Tip: If you are over 75, the TSA will not ask you to remove your shoes or light jacket.)

Get Ready for Special Screenings

Travelers using wheelchairs, mobility aids, and other medical devices still need to go through the airport screening process. TSA screeners will inspect and physically screen wheelchairs and scooters. You will need to put smaller mobility aids, such as walkers, through the X-ray machine.

If you use a prosthetic limb or wear a medical device such as an insulin pump, you will need to tell the TSA screener. You may be asked to undergo a wand inspection or pat-down, but you will not need to remove your medical device. Be ready to ask for a private inspection if the TSA screeners need to see your device. Familiarize yourself with TSA rules and processes for screening passengers with medical conditions and disabilities so you know exactly what to expect and what to do if your screening officer does not follow established procedures.

Bring Your Common Sense

Approach the airport screening process with a common-sense, positive attitude. Stay alert, particularly as you place carry-on items into plastic bins and while you pick up your bags and put on your shoes. Thieves frequent airport security areas in order to take advantage of the confusion at the outbound end of the screening lane. Repack your laptop and organize your carry-on bag before you put your shoes on so you can keep track of your valuables. Be polite and stay positive throughout the screening process; cheerful travelers tend to get better service. Don't make jokes; TSA officials take references to bombs and terrorism very seriously.

资料来源：https://www.tripsavvy.com/prepare-for-airport-security-screenings-2973039

Unit Seventeen
The Problem of Airline Punctuality

Text

Passage

If you're a seasoned traveler, you've almost certainly experienced the frustration of a delayed flight. After carefully planning a vacation or business trip, you've arrived at the airport early only to find that your flight's departure will be an hour (or several hours) late. It happens all the time. In fact, it's so commonplace that an airport's performance is considered acceptable if only 80 percent of its flights depart on time.

The survey of civil aviation passengers shows that almost all passengers regard the airline punctuality as the most valuable component of the airline. The problem of the airline punctuality has become a definitely crucial factor affecting the products of the airlines.

A flight delay is when an airline flight takes off and/or lands later than its scheduled time. The Federal Aviation Administration(FAA) considers a flight to be delayed when it is 15 minutes later than its scheduled time. A cancellation occurs when the airline does not operate the flight at all for a certain reason.

Flight delays not only bring some losses to the airlines but also to the passengers. In the United States, the FAA estimates that flight delays cost airlines $22 billion yearly. Airlines are forced to pay federal authorities when they hold planes on the tarmac for more than three hours for domestic flights or more than four hours for international flights. Flight delays are inconvenient to passengers. For passengers, the cost of flight delay may be expensive, because it will cause them to delay their personal plans and trips. A passenger who is delayed on a multi-plane trip could miss a connecting flight. Anger and frustration can occur in delayed passengers.

There are quite a lot of factors that cause flight delays. Aircraft turn around requires completing a lot of works in a short time, such as refueling, cleaning, catering, etc. If the work is not completed before the planned take off time, the delay will occur. The easiest way to avoid aircraft turn around delays is to extend turn around time when setting a timetable, so that there is enough time to finish all the necessary work. However, this will have a high-cost impact on the effective use of the aircraft, because this is at the expense of many passengers' favored take off time. Meanwhile, the airline also needs to apply for the new take off and landing time to the Airport Scheduling Committee. So the best solution is for the airline to come up with measures to avoid delays. For an airline that needs to handle its own apron service, it is necessary to ensure that there are plenty of equipments and staff at the peak times, which means that it will increase the cost. It is also a wise and effective way to avoid extreme peak times while arranging timetables. In addition, if the staff can handle the principle of flexible maneuver and do any work that needs to be done, it will greatly shorten the time of turn around. However, this is at the expense of paying expensive wages. For an airline that entrusts a service agent to complete the apron service, ensuring punctuality is relatively easy, if there are multiple agents to choose from.

If all passengers have not completed the boarding procedures, or though they have gone through the boarding procedures, they do not have enough time to go to the boarding gate due to too late processing time, the dispatch of the flight may be delayed. If the baggage of the passengers is not loaded in the cargo hold on time, the delay will also occur. All these problems can be mitigated by the extension of the airline boarding procedures in theory. However, this may cause the airline to face competitive pressures, and it may be difficult for passengers to comply with the extended boarding procedures. Maybe another effective way is to hire more employees and more counters, but this approach is much more expensive and is not feasible in many airports, because the number of the check-in counters assigned to each airlines by the airport is limited. If it is possible to automate the passengers' boarding and the baggage sorting process, the delay will be greatly alleviated. This is also a good way to reduce costs.

Uncooperative weather can be a travel nightmare for airlines and passengers. Snow, rain, fog and wind can delay or cancel flights altogether. Trying to fly an airplane in dense fog is difficult because of the reduction to visibility, especially for high-traffic airports. Strong winds can be dangerous for planes trying to take off or land. The biggest problem is head or tail winds that can affect the overall speed of an aircraft at a time when its speed is critical for a safe take off or landing. Much like the mid-latitude locations near waters can produce wind problems for aircraft, these characteristics also make these areas vulnerable to snowstorms. Snow and ice will reduce visibility, make runways slippery and can affect the way crucial equipment operates. Thunderstorms are prone to have strong winds and visibility-reducing rains. The atmosphere around a thunderstorm can add to turbulence in the air, but most planes are equipped for protection against lightning strikes.

In addition to the above reasons, the factors such as mechanical or maintenance problems, air traffic congestion, crew or pilot issues, security problems or mandatory evacuations, airline or airport errors, limited runway space, ripple effects due to other delayed flights, also affect a flight's arrival and departure schedule.

New words

1. punctuality [ˌpʌŋktʃʊ'ælətɪ] n. 准时，正点
2. seasoned ['si:znd] adj. 经验丰富的

3. frustration [frʌ'streɪʃn] n. 懊丧，懊恼，沮丧；挫折
4. commonplace ['kɒmənpleɪs] adj. 常见的，普遍的；陈腐的
5. frustration [frʌ'streɪʃn] n. 挫折；挫败；失意
6. turnaround ['tɜ:nəraʊnd] n.（飞机等）卸货、加油、服务、重新装货所需时间
7. timetable['taɪmteɪbl] n. 交通工具的运行时间表，时刻表
8. flexible ['flɛksəbl] adj. 能适应新情况的；灵活的；可变动的
9. maneuver [mə'nuvə] n. 策略，谋略，花招
10. mitigate['mɪtɪgeɪt] vt. 使缓和，使减轻；使平息
11. feasible ['fi:zəbl] adj. 可行的；可用的；可实行的；可能的
12. automate ['ɔ:təmeɪt] vt.&vi.（使）自动化；使自动操作
13. alleviate [ə'li:vieɪt] vt. 减轻，缓和
14. nightmare ['naɪtmeə(r)] n. 噩梦；<口>可怕的事情，无法摆脱的恐惧
15. dense [dens] adj. 密集的，稠密的；浓密的，浓厚的
16. visibility ['vɪzə'bɪləti] n. 能见度；可见性
17. vulnerable ['vʌlnərəbl] adj. 脆弱的；易受攻击的
18. congestion [kən'dʒestʃ(ə)n] n. 阻塞；塞车
19. mandatory ['mændət(ə)ri] adj. 强制性的；托管的
20. ripple ['rɪpl] n. 涟漪；波纹

Phrases and expressions

1. civil aviation 民用航空
2. flight delay 航班延误
3. international flight 国际航班
4. connecting flight 衔接航班
5. planned take-off time 计划起飞时间
6. peak time 高峰期
7. cargo hold 货舱
8. boarding procedure 登机手续
9. check-in counter 值机台，办理登机手续的柜台
10. traffic congestion 交通拥堵

Abbreviation

FAA Federal Aviation Administration 美国联邦航空管理局

Notes

1. Airlines are forced to pay federal authorities when they hold planes on the tarmac for more than three hours for domestic flights or more than four hours for international flights.

如果国内航班的班机在停机坪上停留超过 3 个小时或国际航班的班机在停机坪上停留超过 4 个小时，航空公司将不得不向联邦当局支付费用。

2. If all passengers have not completed the boarding procedures, or though they have gone through the boarding procedures, they do not have enough time to go to the boarding gate due to too late processing time, the dispatch of the flight may be delayed.

如果所有旅客没有完成登机手续，或已办理登机手续，但由于办理得太晚，他们没有足够的时间登机，航班就会延误。

3. Maybe another effective way is to hire more employees and more counters, but this approach is much more expensive and is not feasible in many airports, because the number of the check-in counters assigned to each airlines by the airport is limited.

也许另一种有效的方法是雇佣更多的雇员和租用更多的柜台，但这种方法要昂贵得多，在许多机场是不可行的，因为机场分配给每个航空公司的值机柜台的数量是有限的。

Exercises

I. Translate the following phrases into Chinese.

1. check-in counter
2. baggage allowance
3. carry-on baggage
4. oversize baggage
5. checked baggage
6. Declaration Channel
7. Non-Declaration Channel
8. departure registration card
9. Bureau de Change
10. Departure Lounge
11. boarding pass
12. security check

II. Answer the following questions based on the text.

1. What is a flight delay?
2. Do flight delays only bring some losses to the passengers?
3. When does an aircraft turnaround delay occur?
4. What is the easiest way to avoid aircraft turnaround delays?
5. What will happen if all passengers have not completed the boarding procedures, or though they have gone through the boarding procedures, they do not have enough time to go to the boarding gate due to too late processing time?

Supplementary Reading Material

Hong Kong Airlines ranked most punctual airline in Asia; second globally in 2017

HONG KONG, Jan. 8, 2018 /PRNewswire/ — Hong Kong Airlines has been recognised for its excellent On-Time Performance (OTP), having been ranked by UK-based air travel intelligence company OAG as Asia's most punctual airline, and the second globally in 2017.

According to the "OAG Punctuality League 2018" report, which delivers the most updated statistics for airlines based on full year data in 2017, Hong Kong Airlines achieved an OTP rating of 88.83% — a significant increase as compared to 74.46% in 2016.

Hong Kong Airlines operates out of one of the world's busiest air hubs. To maintain its operational efficiency and strive towards OTP excellence, Hong Kong Airlines has always been exploring ways to improve overall flight punctuality. The move to the then newly built Midfield Concourse at Hong Kong International Airport in late 2015 presented an opportunity, as the 105,000 square-metre, five-storey facility provided 20 dedicated parking stands that would serve Hong Kong Airlines well. Currently, over 99% of Hong Kong Airlines' flights out of Hong Kong arrive and depart from the Midfield Concourse, which has become a significant contributing factor to the airline's improved OTP.

Flight information is shared with relevant parties in a timely manner to allow better management of the airport's parking bay occupancy, which in turn provides Hong Kong Airlines with more accurate and efficient bay assignments.

Moreover, Hong Kong Airlines has also set up a dedicated working group to closely monitor its OTP. In the event of a delay, the group would analyse the factors and causes involved in order to determine the root cause. Subsequently, this would allow the airline to implement new processes that help mitigate the chance of similar delays from occurring again.

Moving forward, Hong Kong Airlines remains committed in continually improving the punctuality of its flights to ensure that its passengers arrive at their destination on time. The expansion of the airline's global network has already seen it implement several improvements aimed at streamlining processes, and Hong Kong Airlines is confident that such measures will further enhance its operational efficiency, which will in turn benefit its customers.

About Hong Kong Airlines

Established in 2006, Hong Kong Airlines is a full-service airline firmly rooted in Hong Kong. The airline flies to nearly 40 destinations across Asia Pacificand North America and also maintains codeshare and interline agreements with 95 airline partners. Hong Kong Airlines operates an all-Airbus fleet, comprising of 35 aircraft with an average age of around five years. The airline will progressively take delivery of 21 Airbus A350 aircraft. Since 2011, Hong Kong Airlines has been awarded the four-star rating by Skytrax. Hong Kong Airlines has also been recognised for its excellent On-Time Performance, having been ranked by air travel intelligence company OAG as one of the world's most punctual carriers in 2017.

资料来源：http://www.asiaone.com/business/hong-kong-airlines-ranked-most-punctual-airline-in-asia-second-globally-in-2017

Unit Eighteen

Hijacking

Text

Passage

Hijacks can be classified into four main types, depending on whether they are carried out by military-trained terrorist commandos, political groups using violence, political refugees, or mentally unstable individuals.

All are dangerous, because they are using the most valuable asset in our democracies, human life, to pressure governments or establishments to concede to their demands.

Hijacking is a form of blackmail. Conventional blackmail is often aimed at individuals because of their wealth or status, whereas hijacking is the random taking of anonymous passengers and crews as hostages. The fact that the entire travelling public from the top executive to the family of modest means on an inclusive tour can be (and are) affected mobilizes public opinion. Everybody feels concerned: it could happen to yourself or your family.

"Hijacking could stop tomorrow if governments wished so." An IATA director once declared but before we leave the responsibility of preventing and acting against hijacking to states alone, we will look into the procedures that some airlines have developed to complement if not supplement local authorities' security. Some of these airlines are using so-called sky marshals or armed security officers, sometimes on all flights, sometimes only on high-security flights generally originating in or bound for sensitive areas. Some of these airlines are doing this in cooperation with the state's police or security services, others are doing so on their own initiative as an airline, while hiring and training their own security agents.

In addition to sky marshals, airlines are also developing anti-hijacking methods such as crew training and specially designed cockpit access. The Israeli EI-AI is probably the leading airline in that respect but, understandably, keeps its knowledge very confidential.

Airport authorities are also very involved in hijack prevention. In fact the ICAO recommendations on aviation security (contained in ICAO Annex 17) stress the importance of airport security.

Today the six main technical methods used in airport security are:

1. X-ray luggage screening
2. Metal detector gateway
3. Explosives detectors

4. Psychological detection
5. Sterile areas
6. Dogs

None of these airport prevention methods is completely effective, as the latest hijacks of 1983-1984 demonstrates, seeing that most of them originated from airports equipped with modern devices.

Let us see what governments do when dealing with hijacks.

Basically, governments confronted with hijacked aircraft use three methods:

1. Refusing the aircraft entry into their airspace and /or landing in their country, thus transferring the problem to another country.
2. Negotiating to have hostages released and hijackers surrender.
3. Using special police or military units to storm the aircraft.

International Civil Aviation Organization(ICAO)

The primary objective of the International Civil Aviation Organisation Aviation Security (ICAO Avsec) programme is to assure the safety of passengers by first attempting to deny offenders access to aircraft.

With this objective, the most important element recognised by ICAO is the inspection and screening of passengers and their luggage, and therefore its first action was to establish an aviation security programme in each ICAO contracting state.

The recommendations contained in ICAO Annex 17 (Security) define the basic actions which a state should take as follows:

1. To co-operate with other states and ICAO in exchanging and supplying information regarding aviation security.
2. To prevent the unauthorised entry of weapons and explosives into aircraft by search and screening procedures.
3. To isolate and keep under surveilance the airside of aerodromes.
4. To require of its own airlines to adopt a security programme.
5. To transmit all relevant information to all overfly and destination states, when dealing with a hijacked aircraft.
6. To adopt measures for the safety of passengers and crew of hijacked aircraft, until their journey is terminated.

New words

1. classify ['klæsifai] v. 把……分类
2. commando [kə'mɑːndəu] n. 突击队（员）
3. refugee [refju(:)'dʒiː] n. 避难者，难民

4. asset ['æset] n. 财产，宝贵的人（或物）
5. establishment ['istæbliʃm(ə)nt] n. 行政机构，企业，公司
6. concede [kən'si:d] v. 让步，让与，承认
7. blackmail ['blækmeil] n.&v. 敲诈，勒索
8. conventional [kən'venʃ(ə)n(ə)l] adj. 传统的，惯例的
9. random ['rændəm] adj. 随便的，任意的
n. 偶然的（或随便的）行动
10. anonymous [ə'nɒniməs] adj. 无名的，不知名的
11. hostage ['hɒstidʒ] n. 人质；抵押品
12. mobilize ['məubəlaiz] v. 动员；组织起来
13. marshal ['mɑ:ʃ(ə)l] n. 市警察局长；元帅
14. security [si'kjuərəti] n. 安全，安全防卫措施
15. originate [ə'ridʒineit] v. 始发，发源，引起
16. initiative [i'niʃiətiv] n. 积极性，主动
17. confidential [kɒnfi'denʃ(ə)l] adj. 机密的，秘密的
18. involve [in'vɒlv] v. 包含，含有，卷入
19. prevention [pri'venʃən] n. 预防，防止，制止
20. annex [ə'nɛks] n. 附录；附属建筑物
21. screen [skri:n] v. 甄别；审查
n. 屏幕，隔板
22. psychological [saikə'lɒdʒik(ə)l] adj. 心理（上）的
23. detection [di'tekʃ(ə)n] n. 探测，检波
24. explosive [ik'spləusiv] n. 炸药
25. sterile ['sterail] adj. 无菌的，消过毒的
26. effective [i'fektiv] adj. 有效的，生效的
27. negotiate [ni'gəuʃieit] v. 谈判，协商
28. confront [kən'frʌnt] v. 使面临，使遭遇
29. objective [əb'dʒektiv] n. 目标，目的
30. offender [ə'fendə] n. 罪犯，冒犯者
31. search [sɜ:tʃ] v.&n. 搜寻，搜查
32. surveillance [sə:'veiləns] n. 监视，监督
33. terminate ['tɜ:mineit] v. 结束，终止

Phrases and expressions

1. military-trained terrorist commando 受过军事训练的恐怖分子突击队（员）
2. political group (refugee) 政治团体（避难者）

3. mentally unstable individual 精神不稳定的人
4. inclusive tour 包价旅游
5. public opinion 舆论
6. to look into 调查，研究
7. armed security officer 武装保安人员
8. sky marshal 空中警察
9. sensitive area 敏感地区
10. security agents 保安人员
11. explosive detectors 炸药探测器
12. psychological detection 心理探测法
13. to confront with 面临，对抗
14. special police 特种警察
15. contracting state 缔约国
16. to adopt measures 采取措施

Notes

1. ... originating in or bound for sensitive areas
……来往于敏感地区

2. ... keeps its knowledge very confidential
……它们的做法极端机密

3. To isolate and keep under surveillance the airside of aerodromes
将机场的飞行区与其他地区隔开并处于监视之下

Exercises

I. Translate these special terms into Chinese and learn by heart.

1. stowaway: A person who boards the aircraft illegally and attempts to hide somewhere on board for the purpose of getting a free ride to his destination. Flight service personnel check the aircraft for stowaways at the beginning of each flight.

2. High Season / Low Season: Terms used for fare calculations on some airlines. High season is the period of heavy travel and higher fares. Low season is the period of light travel and lower fares.

3. Jet Lag: The condition in which the body has not yet caught up with the change in time after a flight through several time zones. After a flight from New York to Tokyo, for example, the traveler suddenly finds himself on a schedule that is twelve hours ahead of what it was at his point of departure. He will usually be hungry and sleepy on the basis of New York time, not Tokyo time, and he will suffer some temporary dysfunction. This might last several days before the body has a

chance to overcome the lag or catching up period that is caused by the time difference.

II. Read and analyze the following passages grammatically.

1. The aviation security system inspects and provides security for every one of those flights at every one of those airports and for every one of those passengers and every piece of their carry-on baggage for every flight, at every airport, every day.

2. The US civil aviation security program today is considered the best in the world. The concern about terrorism is real and the airline security programs are undergoing intense scrutiny by the government, by the news media by passengers, and by the public. The depth of that scrutiny and the continuity of that scrutiny are unprecedented.

3. The airlines, the airport operators, and the aviation industry in general treat this very, very seriously. Airline security is synonymous with airline safety. In talking about acts of hijacking, sabotage, terrorism, and terms are synonymous. So the airlines treat security just as they do safety. There is no cutting of corners. Security and safety are paramount in airline operations. To have an unsafe operation or an insecure operation is unthinkable. It can not stand the test of our society.

III. Answer the following questions based on the text.

1. How many types of hijacks can be classified? What are they?
2. What do these airline do against hijacking?
3. What are the main technical methods used in airport security today?
4. What kinds of methods do these governments confronted with hijacked aircraft use?
5. What do the recommendations contained in ICAO Annex 17 (security) define?

Supplementary Reading Material

10 Points to Remember in a Hijacking

Nothing can quite prepare one for the trauma of a hijacking, however, there are a few things one could do in the event of a hijacking, particularly when there are children around.

How to avoid hijackings.

- Be vigilant when pulling out of your driveway or coming home - 68% of all hijackings occur close to home.
- If you suspect you are being followed, slow down at least two to three houses prior to your home to force the vehicle behind you to pass.
- If you have an electric gate, do not pull into your driveway before opening the gate. Rather open your gate while your car is still on the road to allow a quick getaway if necessary.

- If you do not have an electric gate and your child is in the car, take the ignition key with you as you stop to open the gate. The key is a valuable negotiating tool – the criminals want your car and you want your child.
- Don't fall for the "tap tap" trap where the driver of another vehicle gently drives into the back of your car in traffic. Never get out of your car to assess the damage but rather drive to a busy location. Signal to the other driver to follow you. If it is not legitimate they will seldom follow you.

What to do if you are hijacked

- The first and golden rule: Don't antagonize the hijackers. Show them you are not a threat.
- Lift up your arms to show you have no weapon.
- Use your left arm to undo your seatbelt and put your car in neutral.
- Do not turn off your car.
- If you are hijacked while your children are in the car, climb out of the vehicle slowly and tell the hijackers calmly that you need to take your children out. (Remember that the eldest child should always be seated behind the driver and the younger child to the left). Move to the back door directly behind the driver's door. Place one foot firmly in the car, on the floor behind the driver's seat, as you lean across to retrieve the youngest child. The eldest child will probably cling to you and you can get both children out of the car at once.
- Stay calm. If the hijackers panic and the vehicle starts moving before you have your children out of the car, your firm footing in the vehicle will throw your body weight into the car with your children, as opposed to you being left behind and the hijackers speeding off with your children.
- Do not turn your back on the hijackers – your organs are most exposed from the back.
- Avoid direct eye contact with the hijackers.

10 Points to Remember in a Hijacking

Hints are helpful to protect yourself and your family in the event of a hijacking. Criminals prey on ignorance! Be aware and informed.

- Always be alert near gates, driveways or garages and look out for suspicious persons, vehicles and loiterers when leaving or arriving at your home or business.
- Be on the look-out for suspicious people when stopping at stop signs or traffic lights, or while driving in city traffic, especially in quiet areas or at night.
- Drive away quickly if someone suspicious approaches your stationary vehicle.
- Always keep your vehicle doors locked and windows closed. Keep valuables out of sight.
- Don't respond to people indicating that there is something wrong with your vehicle

whilst you are driving. Drive to the nearest garage or safe place, such as a police station.

- If your vehicle breaks down, if possible, drive on to a safe place. Do not wait for other motorists to come to your assistance. Use your cellular phone to contact emergency services for assistance.
- Beware of people asking for directions, especially in parking areas.
- Make sure that you are not followed to and from your home or business, and if you are followed, go to the nearest police station or place where there are many people. Avoid quiet streets or areas.
- If you are hijacked, try to remember as much details regarding the hijackers as possible, such as vehicle registration numbers, clothing, distinguishing features, etc. Contact emergency services as soon as possible.
- Remember if you are hijacked, don't resist, your life is more valuable than the most expensive car.

These points are based on current trends relating to hijacking in the Johannesburg policing area. For all police emergencies phone 10111 - 24 hours - toll free.

资料来源：http://www.netstar.co.za/content/10-points-remember-hijacking

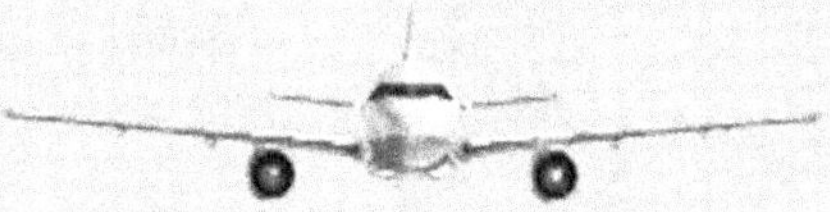

Keys to Exercises

Unit One

I. Write down the full name of each abbreviation and translate it into Chinese.

1. Civil Aviation Administration of China　中国民用航空局
2. Federal Aviation Administration　美国联邦航空局
3. European Aviation Safety Agency　欧洲航空安全局
4. International Air Transport Association　国际航空运输协会
5. International Civil Aviation Organization　国际民航组织
6. Private Pilot Licence　私人飞行执照
7. Commercial Pilot Licence　商用飞机驾驶员执照
8. Aviation Transport Pilot Licence　航空运输执照
9. Instrument Rating　仪表飞行等级
10. Crew Resource Management　机组资源管理

II. Translate the following sentences into English.

1. 译文：Although airplanes can be designed for various purposes, most of them have the same major structure, including fuselage, wings, an empennage, landing gear and a powerplant.

2. 译文：Fuselage is the main body section of an aircraft that carries crew, passengers, cargo, weapon and equipment on board and holds all components of the aircraft together

3. 译文：The wing provides the principal lifting force for an aircraft, which is generated from the dynamic action of the wing with respect to the air.

4. 译文：Flight control surfaces include all those moving surfaces of an airplane which allow a pilot to adjust and control the aircraft's flight attitude

5. 译文：The tail has a fixed horizontal stabilizer and a fixed vertical stabilizer, which help to maintain the stability of an aircraft. The horizontal stabilizer prevents an up-and-down movement of the nose (called pitch), while the vertical stabilizer keeps the nose of the plane from swinging from side to side (called yaw).

III. Read and translate the following short passages into Chinese.

1. 译文：航空器是能够从空气中获得动力的飞行器。它可以利用空气静浮力或空气动力，或在某些情况下利用喷气发动机发出的向下的推力克服自身重力而升空。常见的航空器包括飞机、直升机、飞艇、滑翔机以及热气球。人类作用于航空器的活动叫作航空工业。载人飞机由飞行员在机上操作飞行，而无人飞行器可以通过机载电脑进行远程遥控或自主操作。

2. 译文：C919 是中国首款自主研发的由中国商用飞机有限责任公司制造的中短程双

发窄体客机。机身平滑，设计现代、高效。机上座位数为 158。C919 于 2017 年在上海浦东国际机场完成首次试飞。C919 的成功试飞标志着中国在民航飞机制造业取得了重大突破，并有望在未来打破波音和空客的垄断。

IV. Answer the following questions based on the text.

1. Among all jet planes made by Boeing, the 747 is the largest and is often referred to by its original nickname, "Jumbo Jet". The Boeing 747 is a wide-body commercial jet airliner and cargo aircraft with four engines. It has distinctive hump-like upper deck along the forward part of the aircraft which is to serve as a first class lounge or extra seating or allows the aircraft to be easily converted to a cargo carrier by removing seats and installing a front cargo door. Aircraft of this type can accommodate 366 passengers in a normal configuration. But if converted into all-economy configuration, it can carry up to 490 passengers. First flown commercially in 1970, the 747 held the passenger capacity record for 37 years. The 747-400, the most common variant in service, has a high subsonic cruise speed up to 570 mph with an intercontinental range of 7,260 nautical miles.

2. Generally speaking, there are more seats in economy class cabin than in first class cabin except on some special occasions such as charters. The first class section is the class with the best service, and is typically the highest priced. It is characterized by having a larger amount of space between seats, some of which can even be converted into beds, high quality food and drinks, personalized service and so on. Economy class seats are much cheaper than those of first class simply because the level of comfort is lower. The distance between each seat is short, and there is a smaller variety of food and entertainment.

3. Airline cabin is frequently classified as narrow-body if there is a single aisle with seats on either side like Airbus A320 family and Boeing 737 or wide-body if there are two aisles with a block of seats between them in addition to the seats on the side, such as the Boeing 747 or the Airbus A380.

4. Usually, a seating chart or aircraft seat map will be published for informational purposes or for the passengers to select their seat at booking or check-in, which indicates the basic seating layout, the numbering and lettering of the seats, the location of the emergency exits, lavatories, galleys, bulkheads and wings. There is a seating chart with the passengers' name for the convenience of the flight service crew as well as for record-keeping.

5. The seats on board are marked with letters and numbers. In many planes, the letters begin with "A" on the left side of the cabin, with the highest letter on the rightmost side. For medium-sized and small aircraft, the numbers of the seats usually begin with "one" at the front part for first class and at the rear part for economy. And the largest number will appear at the bulkhead that separates the two sections. Some airlines may mark the seats with the names of the passengers in first class cabin.

Unit Two

I. Analyze the following passages grammatically.

1. 转折关系复合句。

2. 时间状语从句，原因状语从句，非限制性定语从句。

II. Answer the following questions based on the text.

1. When the aircraft approaches the speed of sound, the alarm signals for the air ahead become shorter, giving the molecules less time to get out of the way. The compressed molecules form into a severer vertical shockwave as the aircraft reaches the speed of sound. Its pressure increases instantaneously, so in the vicinity of the source it sounds like the crackling bullwhip.

2. Once the aircraft speeds up over Mach 1, the shock wave forms a cone. As the apex of the cone, the aircraft drags it forward. Because only at the high altitude can supersonic flight be achieved, there is ample time for the shock wave to enlarge significantly before it gets to the ground. Finally, near the ground we hear a muffled rumble by the weakened shockwave.

3. A supersonic transport (SST) is a civilian supersonic aircraft designed to transport passengers at speeds greater than the speed of sound.

4. The cabin windows of SST are designed smaller so as to reduce the probability of in the highly pressurized cabin.

5. To date, the only SSTs to see regular service have been Concorde and the Tupolev Tu-144.

Unit Three

III. Answer the following questions based on the text.

1. The flight deck is designed to allow both pilots to reach all the essential controls and switches without moving from their seats. There may be up to 150 instruments.

2. Pilots rarely concentrate on one particular instrument.

3. Aviation's standard arrangement of the four principal readings, showing speed, height, attitude and heading.

4. Aviation has its traditions. In the early years, influenced by the keep right rules of the road and at sea, aircraft also kept right on the airways. For ease of visibility captains chose to sit on the left.

5. Red or yellow illuminated squares accompanied by loud buzzing indicate immediately any failure of any part of the aircraft and its control systems. The strident sound of 18 different warning signals could disturb the serenity of a flight deck. All airlines may shortly adopt a feature at present only used in some civil airliners and military aircraft-electronic head up display (HUD).

Unit Four

I. Translate the following words or phrases into English.

1. galley
2. escape slide
3. seat belt
4. first aid kit
5. extinguisher
6. tray table
7. grab handle/ armrest
8. oxygen mask
9. reading light
10. call button
11. flight attendant
12. passenger manifest
13. life vest
14. ditching
15. water evacuation
16. terminal
17. aero bridge/ jetway
18. purser
19. lavatory/ toilet
20. window-shade/ sunshade
21. window seat
22. aisle seat
23. overhead compartment
24. emergency exit
25. passenger step/ passenger stairs/ stairs vehicle

II. Read and translate the following short passages into Chinese.

1. 译文：在航空领域，疲劳已成为飞行中备受关注的一个问题。除了繁重的工作和特殊的工作环境（较高的高度、低气压、低氧分压、噪声、震动等），乘务人员还要承担不规律的工作日程、长时间的工作、时差、夜班等，这些与人体的生理规律相冲突，并造成了睡眠缺乏、疲劳、健康和安全等各种问题。

2. 译文：在一架客机的飞行中，各种外界因素影响着乘客的舒适感，其中包括诸如温度、噪声、空气质量、灯光等环境条件。人们根据这些因素制定了相应的标准以确保飞行中的各种因素不会对乘客的健康造成不利影响。根据一项最新的研究，彩色灯光也可以用来在乘客中刻意创造出一种舒适感。研究指出，彩色的灯光可以影响人对于温度的感知。不同的光可以使人感觉环境温度要比实际更温暖或者更凉爽，从而为乘客提供一种温度上的舒适感。

3. 译文：座椅通常会配备一些设施。飞机客舱内的座椅可以通过机械（通常在经济舱以及短程头等舱或商务舱）或者电动的方式（通常在远程头等舱或商务舱）进行调整使其倾斜从而为乘客提供更好的舒适度。大多数飞机都装备了可用于餐饮和阅读的小桌板。在多数经济舱里这些桌板大都是折叠于座椅背侧。而在大多数头等舱、商务舱、飞机隔板座位处、紧急逃生出口座位处，这些小桌板是折叠放置于扶手中的。在每个座舱座椅的背后，通常有一个口袋，里面盛放着杂志和安全说明书供乘客在飞行中阅读。

III. Answer the following questions based on the text.

1. A crucial factor that affects the revenue of an airline is the configuration of the aircraft cabin. The more passengers an airplane can carry, the more profits will be generated to the airline.

2. In the early development stage of commercial passenger-carrying aviation, aircraft could carry only a small number of passengers. For instance, the Fokker F.II had an enclosed accommodation for four passengers, with a fifth seat alongside the pilot in his unenclosed cockpit which was originally intended for a mechanic or navigator. The Fokker F.III could carry only five passengers. And the Fokker F. XII had a capacity of 16 passengers.

3. To cater for passengers' need for slumber, reclining seating and bunks were installed in DC-7.

4. Airbus A320 family has rows of six seats with a 3+3 layout. The CRJ series have 1+2 seating arrangement and Douglas DC9 is featured 2+3 seating. Very wide planes such as Boeing 747 or the Airbus A380 have rows of ten seats, typically in a 3+4+3 layout.

5. In many commercial flights, there are first-class, business class and economy class cabins for passengers with different needs.

Unit Five

I. Write down the full name of each abbreviation and translate it into Chines.

1. Baby Meal 婴儿餐
2. Child Meal 儿童餐
3. Moslem Meal 穆斯林餐；清真餐
4. Hindu Meal 印度餐
5. Kosher Meal 犹太餐
6. Vegetarian Meal 素食餐
7. Diabetic Meal 糖尿病餐
8. Fat Free Meal 无脂肪餐

II. Analyze the following passages grammatically.

1. However 转折连词，large-scale travel 主语，aspiring after speed rather than comfort 分词做定语，need 谓语 a large food and beverage supply 并列宾语。

2. 介宾短语做伴随状语。

III .Answer the following questions based on the text.

1. In order to ensure the taste and texture of food, the food supply may be contracted by large hotels, restaurants or specialized companies.

2. Meals must be loaded on the aircraft 20 to 40 minutes prior to departure.

3. These must usually be ordered in advance, sometimes when buying the ticket.

4. Religious diets, including kosher, halal, and Hindu, Buddhist and Jain vegetarian (sometimes termed Asian vegetarian) meals.

5. To avoid food poisoning at the same time, the captain and the co-pilot usually eat different meals and are banned to eat shellfish.

Unit Six

I. read and explain the following passage.

1. 镭射导航

镭射“陀螺仪”可能很快就会成为导航系统无可替代的重要组成部分，挂载在航空器上的三个镭射“陀螺仪”能监视最微小的运动。它们包含在每个角度都有镜面的三角形导管中。以相对方向传送的两条镭射线花费相同时间传送到三角管附近，但当被飞行器运动扭转时，其中一条射线完成一个环形轨迹需要花费更长时间。

2. 卫星导航系统

已经在轨道上运行的几颗导航卫星，是不断发展的各种卫星系统中的一种。到 19 世纪 90 年代为止被全部运行。它最终的 24 颗卫星，同时在 1 万英里高空的轨道上运行，会提供持续的高质量的定位功能。当其功能良好时，该系统会让坐在 20 英尺宽的波音 747 飞机里的飞行员了解到自己身处何处。

II. Translate the following terms into Chinese.

1. 导航是一门利用地标和设备从某地到其他地方寻找道路的科学。

2. 地面导航辨别方向的基本设备是指南针，它分为两种类型：磁铁指南针和陀螺仪指南针。

3. 配备有导航传送器的轨道卫星，目前能完美地提供定位功能，精确度高达 20 英尺。

4. 归航时依据助航设备飞行，无须风的纠正，调整飞行器航向以便保持相同的相对方位。

III. Analyze the following passages grammatically:

1. 动名词做主语，并列关系。

2. 过去分词做后置定语。

3. 选择关系从句，定语从句。
4. 并列关系，定语从句。
5. 方式状语从句。

Unit Seven

I. Write down the full name of each abbreviation and translate it into Chinese.

1. Instrument Landing System	仪表着陆系统
2. Instrument Guidance System	仪表引导系统
3. Very High Frequency Omnidirectional Range	甚高频全方向信标
4. Non-directional Beacon	无方向信标
5. Distance Measuring Equipment	测距仪
6. Precision Approach Radar	精密进近雷达
7. Airport Surveillance Radar	机场监视雷达
8. Global Positioning System	全球定位系统
9. Global Navigation Satellite System	全球卫星导航系统
10. Regional Navigation	区域导航
11. Required Navigation Performance	所需导航性能
12. Localizer-type Directional Aid	航向道定向设备

II. Try to learn the following position report.

1. 当前位置在航路点 OBLIK，时间为 6 点 46 分，保持飞行高度 310，预计到达航路点 ZF 时间为 6 点 58 分，再下一个位置是航路点 WUH。

2. 当前位置北纬 42 度东经 165 度时间为 8 点，飞行高度 390，预计到达北纬 44 度东经 180 度时间为 9 点，再下一个位置是西经 170 度。

III. Read and translate the following short passages into Chinese.

1. 译文：现代商业飞机的驾驶舱是一个科技奇迹。电脑屏幕和键盘已经取代了老式的开关、按钮和仪表。然而，大多数的商业飞行员仍然携带着过去 70 年里用的皮质的活页夹装的纸质航图。波音公司的一个部门正在开发一种新型的 3D 综合视景技术，希望以打印和电子的形式取代传统的航图。这种系统是一种大型的计算机显示器，展示了飞机周围地形的实景，并提供导航信息。最初，这种系统将可能会出现在公务机的驾驶舱内，并最终应用于商业飞机。

2. 译文：飞机的操纵依赖于基本操纵面，包括副翼、升降舵和方向舵，辅助的操纵面，包括安定面、扰流板和襟翼，以及发动机推力。飞机向各个角度的灵活动作依靠某个或多个操纵面完成。然而，如果飞行员的精力持续用于操纵这些物理操纵面，飞机导航、通信、雷达以及其他特殊设备的应用会受到严重的限制。自动飞行控制和稳定系统减轻了飞行员的工作量，并为飞机在各种速度情况下提供了稳定性。自动飞行控制系统能够在无电线导航的帮助下驾驶飞机，修正风并使飞机不依赖飞行员的辅助进行自动着陆。

IV. Answer the following questions based on the text.

1. NAVAID refers to navigation aid. During flight, the pilot could receive a signal from a ground-stationed NAVAID, through which the pilots could not only realize whether the course is to or from the station, but also he could understand whether the aircraft deviates from the course. Then they could make adjustment to correct the direction.

2. These non-directional radio beacons are sensitive to atmospheric and other types of interferences such as poor signals or the disturbance from other stations, which may cause the malfunction of the instrument on board.

3. INS, LORAN and Decca are three of the common transoceanic navigation systems used in civil aviation.

4. INS refers to Inertial Navigation Systems. It is a self-contained navigation system which requires no external references to determine its position, orientation, or velocity after initialization. Thus it is immune to jamming and deception and suitable for long-range flight over water or land areas without adequate radio station on the ground.

5. GPS means Global Positioning system. It is a space-based radio navigation system with better accuracy than any previous land-based system and available at almost all locations on the Earth. It requires only a few dozen satellites to provide worldwide coverage.

Unit Eight

I. Analyze the following passages grammatically.

1. 时间状语从句。

2. 转折关系。

3. 原因状语从句。

II. Answer the following questions based on the text.

1. The same type of aircraft, which usually takes off in two different directions, has a minimum time interval of one minute. If they take off in the same direction, however, the time interval is two minutes. Producing tail air flow disturbance, a wide-body jet departure usually holds back a light aircraft departure by 10 minutes.

2. From 45,000 to 75,000 feet is the highest altitudes used by supersonic and high-flying commercial jets; below the highest altitudes are the lower airways used by subsonic jets; the altitudes below are usually used by slower turboprop aircraft and aircraft propelled by propeller.

3. Air traffic controllers are personnel responsible for the safe, orderly, and expeditious flow of air traffic in the global air traffic control system. Usually stationed in air traffic control centers and control towers on the ground, they monitor the position, speed, and altitude of aircraft in their assigned airspace visually and by radar, and give directions to the pilots by radio.

4. The default language of aviation world wide is English.

Unit Nine

III. Answer the following questions based on the text.

1. The control tower is the nerve-centre of an airport. At the busiest international centre controller may direct up to 2,000 aircraft movements a day.

2. It may be a small double-decker cabin at a club airfield from which one controller directs aircraft along a single airstrip.

3. Control towers in the large airports have two control rooms. Controllers in the visual control room at the top are responsible for aircraft taking off for aircraft taxing, and for final landing instructions.

4. Approach controllers, working in the orange glow from their radarscopes, guide inbound traffic to the runways.

5. Intense concentration is needed to track dozens of aircraft moving at speed within a small area.

Unit Ten

I. Write down the full name of each abbreviation and translate it into Chinese.

1. Visual Flight Rules	目视飞行规则
2. Instrument Flight Rules	仪表飞行规则
3. Notice to Airman	航行通告
4. Weight and Balance Manual	载重平衡手册
5. Visual Meteorological Conditions	目视气象条件
6. Instrument Meteorological Conditions	仪表气象条件
7. Aerodrome Flight Information Service	机场航行情报服务
8. Aeronautical Information Service	航行情报服务
9. Aviation Weather Service	航空气象服务
10. Civil Air Regulations	民用航空规则

II. Try to explain the following terms with the help of dictionary.

1. It refers to the total weight of the passengers, their luggage and any cargo.

2. It means the basic weight of the aircraft when ready for operation, including crew but excluding any payload or usable fuel.

3. It is the sum of operating weight empty and payload – that is, the laden weight of an aircraft, excluding any usable fuel.

4. It is the weight of an aircraft at the terminal building when ready for departure. This includes the zero fuel weight and all required fuel.

5. It is the weight of an aircraft at the start of a runway, just prior to brake release for

take-off. This is the ramp weight minus any fuel used for taxiing.

6. It is the weight of an aircraft as it takes off partway along a runway.

7. It is the weight of an aircraft as it lands at the destination. This is the brake release weight minus the trip fuel burned. It includes the zero fuel weight, unusable fuel, and all alternate, holding and reserve fuel.

III. Read and translate the following short passages into Chinese.

1. 译文：近些年来，由于生产石油地区数量有限，以及石油资源日益枯竭，可再生能源资源变得日益重要。航空领域中的商业和货物运输对于传统和可替代燃油的需求量不断增长。航空领域中使用的石油衍生产品会影响空气质量。因此必须减少航空业中造成温室气体排放的各种因素。地面车辆所使用的生物燃油也可以应用于航空领域，以便减少燃油成本以及排放物，并促进可持续发展，创造更好的环境。

2. 译文：飞行计划制订者在制订飞行计划时通常要避免特殊用途空域（SUA）。特殊用途空域是指专门用于某种活动的空域，而一般的飞机则被禁止参与该活动。这些活动通常都具有军事性质。大多数的 SUA 空域都在航图上标出来。SUA 空域分为几类，包括限航区、禁航区、军事活动区、警告区、警戒区、临时飞行限制、国家安全区、射击控制区等。例如华盛顿白宫以及古巴上空的区域都属于此类空域。

3. 译文：在制订飞行计划时，还要考虑由于目的地机场的特殊情况，（例如恶劣天气）飞机可以飞到的一个或更多的备降机场。制订计划时，要仔细规划备降场，飞机预计装载的油及其总重量足以使飞机飞到该备降场，并且备降场有能力接收该类型的飞机。除此之外，在目的地或者备降场上空由于天气或交通原因而导致的等待也需要考虑在飞行计划里。如果要考虑到等待的因素，飞行计划中还要写明额外要带的燃油以及等待的时间。

IV. Answer the following questions based on the text.

1. Flights are dispatched in a modernized office equipped with various electronic devices these days and they are dispatched in less than an hour.

2. Critical data about the aircraft itself, departure and arrival points, payload of passengers, freight, luggage and fuel, latest weather changes en route and at the destination will be typed into a computer and several possible routes will be printed out (minimum distance, minimum time, minimum cost). Then the best one is selected.

3. Airplanes fly along designated airways, which can be thought of as three-dimensional highways for aircraft. But they do not necessarily link two cities. Most airways are eight nautical miles (14 kilometers) wide, and the airway flight levels keep aircraft separated by at least 1 000 vertical feet from aircraft on the flight level above and below. They usually intersect at NAVAIDs, which designate the allowed points for changing from one airway to another. Airways have names consisting of one or more letters followed by one or more digits such as R342 or G17.

4. No, apart from the amount of fuel carried to the destination, a contingency amount should also be taken into account in case of diversion, holding, headwind and other emergency situations

in order to ensure flight safety.

5. Sheets of navigation and weather data, notices of conditions at destination and alternate airports, lists of VIPs and CIPs (commercially important people), details of passengers' special requirements as well as the flight plan constitute a great document which needs to be signed by the captain for acceptance and confirmed by the dispatcher.

Unit Eleven

I. Translation the following phrases into Chinese.

1. 航空气象学
2. 航空气象观测
3. 航空区域（天气）预报
4. 航空气象情报
5. 航空气候区划
6. 飞机气象探测
7. 重要气象情报
8. 危险天气通报
9. 机场危险天气警报
10. 国际民航组织标准大气
11. 空中能见度
12. 跑道能见度
13. 跑道积冰
14. 最低气象条件
15. 机场最低气象条件
16. 禁飞天气
17. 明语气象报告
18. 航空气象电码
19. 飞行员气象报告
20. 航空气象保障
21. 机场预约天气报告
22. 飞机天气侦察
23. 对空气象广播
24. 航空（天气）预报
25. 航线（天气）预报
26. 航空天气订正预报
27. 着陆（天气）预报
28. 机场特殊天气报告

29. 高度表拨定（值）
30. 飞机积冰
31. 晴空湍流
32. 飞机颠簸
33. 飞机尾迹
34.（废气）凝结尾迹
35.（废气）蒸发尾迹
36. 飞机尾流
37. 低空风切变
38. 场面气压
39. 顺风
40. 侧风
41. 逆风
42. 航行风
43. 风向袋

II. Analyze the following passages grammatically.

1. 时间状语从句。
2. 原因状语从句，非限制性定语从句。
3. 转折关系。

III. Answer the following questions based on the text.

1. The aircraft de-ice the wings with the hot air from jet engines during take off.

2. Terminal aerodrome forecasts (TAFs) are complied at large airport weather office by meteorologists who know local weather patterns well.

3. They are usually accompanied by strong winds, heavy rain, and sometimes snow, sleet, hail, or, in contrast, no precipitation at all.

4. Unfavorable wind shear may dangerously reduce the aircraft's speed by more than 60mph, so forecasters have to pay close attention to it.

5. Clear-air turbulence (CAT) is the turbulent movement of air masses in the absence of any visual clues such as clouds, and is caused when bodies of air moving at widely different speeds meet. Severe CAT may cause the aircraft to shake obviously and even change altitude, however it does not last long if the pilot could alter flight level.

Unit Twelve

III. Answer the following questions according to the text.

1. Accidents do happen, and when they do, crew training, aircraft equipment and the good sense of the passengers may be fundamental to survival.

2. Cabin crews check that they are fastened at take off and landing, and that babies are installed in special cot-holders.

3. Do not, unless you are well versed in them, ignore the safety demonstrations at the beginning of a flight. Learn how to put on a life jacket, and how to use the emergency oxygen masks stored above the seat or in the back of the seat in front.

4. Never smoke in the toilets where inflammable materials are invariably used in the furnishings. Between 1946 and 1976, 316 accidents were caused by in-flight fires or smoke: many began in the toilets.

5. If doors are inoperative, they activate the emergency exits, ordering passengers to unfasten seat belts, leave everything behind, and make for the designated escape chutes indicated by the cabin staff.

Unit Thirteen

I. Translate the following words or phrases into English.

1. pressurization system
2. air conditioning system
3. hydraulic failure
4. electrical system
5. communication system
6. flight control system
7. fire protection system
8. anti-ice system
9. aircraft condition monitoring system
10. automatic interchange system

II. Read and translate the following short passages into Chinese or English.

1. 译文：今天，很多航空相关领域都遭遇了劳务人员短缺问题。而未来该领域需要更多的技术工人。波音和空客公司的专家预计截至 2031 年航空业将遭遇用工荒，而对于机务维修人员的需求量将达到 600,000 人。近些年，大工程机务维修，也被称作维护、维修和大修活动（MRO）已经外包给外企以便节省成本。然而，尽管预计未来会对劳动力有更大的需求，市场增长以及相应的补偿，仍然少有女性会进入或继续待在飞机维修工作领域。

2. 译文：许多机务维修工作，尤其是大修工程，可能不是由一班人完成的。机务维修工人通常轮流进行工作，一组人完成一部分工作。由于时间短，因此没有时间进行会议交接。而这种情况下，信息交接时的准确性和有效性则成为了维修工作的重中之重。尽管轮班维修对于交流造成了一定困难，但同时也提供了发现和更正错误的机会。在交接工作时下一组工作人员可以发现并及时改正这些问题。

3. 译文：Aircraft maintenance manuals (AMMs) are very important document to ensure the

proper operation of maintenance. The manuals contain important information for continued airworthiness of aircraft. However, the mass text descriptions and static pictures those traditional AMMs have limited their ability to show complicated aircraft structures and maintenance procedures accurately and completely. In order to improve the accuracy and descriptive ability of maintenance manuals, a new style of aircraft maintenance manual, a three-dimensional (3D) maintenance manual, has been developed.

4. 译文：The D check, sometimes known as a "heavy maintenance visit" (HMV) is by far the most comprehensive and demanding check for an airplane. An airliner experiences such check approximately every 6-10 years. It is a check that nearly takes the entire airplane apart for inspection and overhaul. Even the paint on the fuselage metal skin may need to be completely removed for further inspection. This check can usually cost 50,000 man-hours and 2 months, depending on the aircraft itself and the number of technician involved. On average, a commercial aircraft undergoes three D checks before being retired.

III. Answer the following questions based on the text.

1. Aircraft maintenance is the overhaul, repair, inspection or modification of an aircraft or aircraft components. As an indispensible segment of aviation industry, it plays a crucial role in maintaining the good performance an aircraft, improving its ability and ensuring flight safety. It is the most important pre-flight activity.

2. Compile maintenance manuals and Service Bulletins stating the maintenance and servicing of the aircraft and its components and continually update these data based on the feedback of the pilots who drive the aircraft.

3. The periods during which each part of an aircraft must be inspected, the type and degree of the inspection, and the replacement of certain components based on flying hours, numbers of landing and other criteria are all stipulated in the maintenance schedule.

4. The hangers should be big enough to hold a wide-bodied airplane. In a typical hanger, huge stagings, equipped with multi-storey working platforms, lighting, lifts and conveyors, are installed around the aircraft so that each part can be thoroughly checked or repaired by the maintenance personnel.

5. Generally speaking, aircraft undergo light checks at 50-60 flying hours, overnight checks at 300-600 hours and full overhaul every 3,600 flying hours.

Unit Fourteen

II. Analyze the following sentences grammatically.

1. 原因状语从句。
2. 被动语态，原因状语。
3. 让步状语从句，时间状语从句。

III. Answer the following questions based on the text.

1. The earliest aircraft take off and landing sites were grassy fields. The plane could approach at any angle that provided a favorable wind direction.

2. The construction of new airports or addition of runways to existing airports, is often resisted by local residents because of the effect on countryside, historical sites, local flora and fauna.

3. For example, because they often flatten out large areas, they can be susceptible to fog in areas where fog rarely forms. In addition, they generally replace trees and grass with pavement, they often change drainage patterns in agricultural areas, leading to more flooding, run-off and erosion in the surrounding land.

4. Safe, convenient and normal flights are the three elements that the authorities must consider when they plan and operate airports.

Unit Fifteen

I. Read and translate the following passages into Chinese.

1. 快速消防/救援车辆的设计目的是尽管有泡沫和机载设备的重量，仍可与跑车一样快，能加速到每小时 70 英里（112.65 千米）。它携带 200 加仑（240 美制加仑）浓缩的水和泡沫的混合溶液，用于灭火的急救和救援设备，可在主要消防部队到达前保持飞机逃生路线畅通。六轮模型上配有铝制云梯。多功能底盘可以安装担架和其他特殊设备，作用等同于救护车。

2. 重型消防车通过监视器每分钟可排放 9 000 加仑（10 800 美制加仑）的水或泡沫，在前后运动时，通过每个手抓排放 900 加仑（1 080 美制加仑）。

3. 重型机场碰撞机可由单人操作，可运载五人组。它可容纳 3 000 多加仑的水和超过 360 加仑的泡沫，以每小时 60 英里的速度行进。它可抛掷 300 英尺的喷气式飞机。

4. 搜寻和救援是一项寻找失踪飞机并帮助那些发现需要救援的人的服务。

II. Analyse the following sentences grammatically.

1. 时间状语，分词结构做伴随状语。

2. 分词结构做伴随状语。

3. 让步状语从句，转折关系。

4. 时间状语。

5. 过去分词做后置定语，转折关系。

III. Answer the following questions based on the text.

1. Airport fire services will turn out on full emergency stand-by on the slightest indication that something is wrong with a landing plane. They turn out on average once a day at a major airport.

2. Now every major airport is equipped with rapid intervention vehicles (RIVs) in order to reach the runways within two minutes of an alarm. RIVs are fast trucks that carry foam, water,

medical and rescue equipment, and lights for use in fog and darkness.

3. Turret-mounted foam guns ("blabbermouths") swivel to project the foam up to 300 feet.

4. Kerosene is less inflammable than the fuels used by many airlines, but more expensive.

5. Airport fire-fighters wear flame-resistant aluminized clothing and are equipped with breathing apparatus against smoke and the toxic fumes produced by burning aircraft furnishings.

Unit Sixteen

I. Translate the following words or phrases into English.

1. customs inspection counter
2. duty-free goods
3. contraband/ forbidden article/ prohibited items
4. airport public security
5. airport terminal sterile area
6. detection gate/ security gate
7. boarding gate
8. conveyor belt
9. flammable article
10. explosive article
11. corrosive article
12. radioactive article
13. poisonous article
14. liquid article

II. Read and translate the following short passages into Chinese.

1. 译文：炸药追踪探测器是一种能够探测出微量爆炸物的设备。这种设备获取一定的用肉眼看不到的微量物作为样本，探测并分析其中的成分。这种爆炸物探测器是具有高度敏感性，精确性，多用途性，且无须与物体接触的扫描系统。可广泛应用于机场和其他易受非法活动干涉的地方。

2. 译文：狗类灵敏的嗅觉使得它们成为各种安保应用领域的宝贵财富。然而这种用途有时也会有内在的局限性。这就促使人们在过去的十年里研发出一种人工嗅探设备来作为安检的补充手段甚至替代嗅探狗。这种设备也被称作“化学嗅探器”或者“电子鼻”。与嗅探狗一样，这种机器可以探测出残留物，表明有违禁物品的存在或曾接触过违禁物品，例如爆炸物或者毒品。这种设备可以应用于各种场所，如边境地区，机场以及其他重要的安检点。

3. 译文：利用含有乘客个人信息的数据库，诸如全身扫描的技术手段以及更好的信息分享措施以提高航空安全系数。但是这些改变会牵涉对个人隐私的侵犯，也需要政府更有效的监管。这些改变也可以使当局了解旅行者们更多的关于他们个人，家庭以及各种社会关系的情况。鉴于此，旅行者们会被各种仪器以让人难以想象的深入方式进行扫描。而乘客们则需要学会对此习以为常。

III. Answer the following questions based on the text.

1. Because airport is a place with high concentration of people, it becomes a potential target for smuggling, theft, illegal immigration, terrorism and other kinds of crimes.

2. There are many terrorism activities in aviation history, for example, in 1930 a Peruvian Airlines plane was hijacked. The September 11 attack is the most widely recognized event.

3. Airports and airlines at risk may have air cargo X-rayed or as at the Lufthansa terminals, containerized cargo will be decompressed for 12 hours to avoid bomb explosion in cargo holds during flight. Some cargo may have to be stored in a safe place for more than 24 hours or go through some special disposal procedures authorized by aviation authority.

4. Passengers have to undergo a series of security checks since they enter the terminal. They must show their flight ticket, boarding pass, and valid identification, like ID card, passport or certificate of soldiers. Some countries also fingerprint travelers or use Retina and Iris scanning to detect crimes. Besides, scanning facilities including hand-held detectors, metal detectors and full-body scanning machines in which passengers are essentially X-rayed are utilized to check for potential hidden dangerous goods on their persons like explosives, flammable objects, toxic substances, weapons and so on. In some countries, specially trained personnel may engage passengers in a conversation to detect threats rather than solely depending on equipment.

5. Airport security depend on all kinds of advanced equipment which can be used to detect any potential dangerous goods, but eventually it relies on teams of well-trained detection equipment operators as well as experienced security staff.

Unit Seventeen

I. Translate the following phrases into Chinese.

1. 值机柜台
2. 行李重量限额
3. 手提行李
4. 超大行李
5. 托运行李
6. 申报通道
7. 非申报通道
8. 出境登记卡
9. 外币兑换处
10. 候机大厅
11. 登机牌
12. 安全检查

II. Answer the following questions based on the text.

1. A flight delay is when an airline flight takes off and/or lands later than its scheduled time.

2. Flight delays not only bring some losses to the airlines but also to the passengers.

3. Aircraft turn around requires completing a lot of work in a short period of time, such as refueling, cleaning, catering, etc. If the work is not completed before the planned take-off time, the delay will occur.

4. The easiest way to avoid aircraft turn around delays is to extend turn around time when setting a timetable, so that there is enough time to finish all the necessary work.

5. If all passengers have not completed the boarding procedures, or though they have gone through the boarding procedures, they do not have enough time to go to the boarding gate due to too late processing time, the dispatch of the flight may be delayed.

Unit Eighteen

I. Translate these special terms into Chinese and learn by heart.

1. 偷渡者是指自然人违反出入国（边）境管理法规，在越过国界线或者通过法律上的拟制国界时，不从指定口岸通行或者不经过边防检查，或者未经出境许可、未经入境许可，可追究其行政责任或者刑事责任的行为。偷越国（边）境是违法行为。

2. 买飞机票旺季或淡季：每年的 3～6 月和 10～12 月底是旺季，其他月份均为淡季。除上述原因外，还有一种原因是决定飞机票价格高低的因素，即：往返时间长短。即：超过半个月的往返飞机票，肯定比往返十天八天的票价要高；反过来就是，往返十天八天的飞机票肯定比往返半个月以上的票价要低。

3. 地方时：随地球自转，一天中太阳东升西落，太阳经过某地天空的最高点时为此地的地方时 12 时，因此，不同经线上具有不同的地方时。同一时区内所用的同一时间是区时（本区中央经线上的地方时），全世界所用的同一时间是世界时(零度经线的地方时)。区时经度每 15 度差 1 小时，地方时经度每 1 度差 4 分钟。

各地的标准时间为格林威治时间（G.M.T）加上（+）或减去（-）时区中所标的小时和分钟数时差。许多国家还采用夏令时（DST），如美国每年 4 月到 9 月实行夏令时，时间提前 1 小时。

时差的计算方法：两个时区标准时间（即时区数）相减就是时差，时区的数值大的时间早。比如中国是东八区（+8），美国东部是西五区（-5），两地的时差是 13 小时；北京比纽约要早 13 个小时;如果是美国实行夏令时的时期，相差 12 小时。

II. Read and analyse the following passages grammatically.

1. 并列关系从句。

2. 第一句话是主要观点，后面几句是解释支持论点。

3. 从正面解释支撑论点——概括总论点——从反面解释支撑论点。

III. Answer the following questions based on the text.

1. Hijacks can be classified into four main types, depending on whether they are carried out by military-trained terrorist commandos, political groups using violence, political refugees, or mentally unstable individuals.

2. Some of these airlines are using so-called sky marshals or armed security officers, sometimes on all flights, sometimes only on high-security flights generally originating in or bound for sensitive areas. Some of these airlines are doing this in cooperation with the state's police or security services, others are doing so on their own initiative as an airline, while hiring and training their own security agents.

3. Today the six main technical methods used in airport security are: X-ray luggage screening, Metal detector gateway, Explosives detectors, Psychological detection, Sterile areas, and Dogs.

4. Basically, governments confronted with hijacked aircraft use three methods:1) Refusing the aircraft entry into their airspace and /or landing in their country, thus transferring the problem to another country. 2) Negotiating to have hostages released and hijackers surrender. 3) Using special police or military units to storm the aircraft.

5. The recommendations contained in ICAO Annex 17 (Security) define the basic actions which is a state should take as follows: 1) To co-operate with other states and ICAO in exchanging and supplying information regarding aviation security. 2) To prevent the unauthorized entry of weapons and explosives into aircraft by search and screening procedures. 3) To isolate and keep under surveillance the airside of aerodromes. 4) To require of its own airlines to adopt a security programme. 5) To transmit all relevant information to all overfly and destination states, when dealing with a hijacked aircraft. 6) To adopt measures for the safety of passengers and crew of hijacked aircraft, until their journey is terminated.

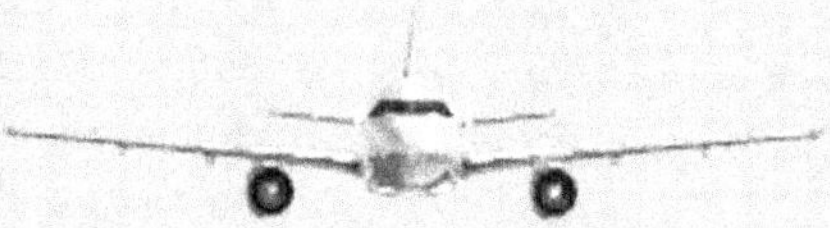

Translations

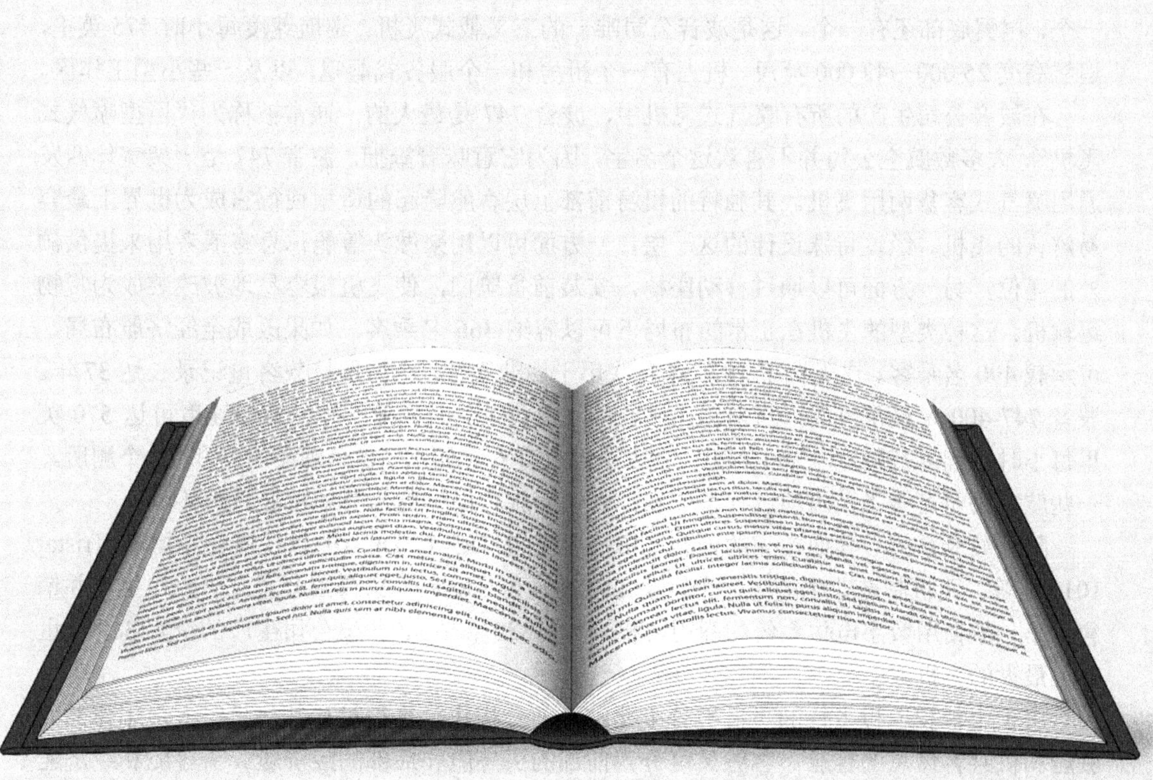

参考译文

第一课　现代飞机简介

如今，飞机已经成为最重要的交通方式之一。尽管飞机类型各异，但这些由航空业中不同制造商生产的飞机都具有共同的标准。有些小公司，特别是在区域运输和通航领域，仍在使用螺旋桨飞机。然而，国际航空公司的所有航班几乎都使用喷气式飞机。

不同类型的飞机在大小、结构、配置、载客量、性能等方面有所差异。这些差异可以通过由制造商设定的一系列型号进行辨别。例如，波音 707 是第一架在商业上取得成功的喷气式客机。该飞机为中型、长航程、窄体、四发喷气客机。根据其不同型号，载客量可达到 140～219 人，航程 2 500～5 750 海里（1 海里=1.852 千米）。巡航速度 470 节（1 节=1 海里/时=1.852 千米/时），最大航程 5 757 英里（1 英里=1.609 千米）。平均飞行高度为 25 000～40 000 英尺（1 英尺=0.304 8 千米）。机上有两套厨房，头等舱和经济舱各一套。另外，还有两个辅助厨房。位于飞机前部的头等舱乘客休息室。

与 707 相比，波音 727 相对较小，主要用于短程和中短程飞行。载客量为 149～189 人。最新型的波音 727 可以不间断飞行 2 700 海里。该飞机有三个发动机，在机身后侧左右各一个，尾翼底部还有一个。这是波音公司唯一的三叉戟式飞机。巡航速度每小时 575 英里，巡航高度 25 000～42 000 英尺。机上有一个厨房和一个服务式酒吧，以及一些小型工作区。

在波音公司生产的所有喷气式飞机中，波音 747 是最大的，通常被称为“巨型喷气式飞机”。大多数航空公司并不喜欢这个名字，因为它意味着笨拙。波音 747 是一架宽体四发通用喷气式客货两用飞机。其独特的机身前部上层客舱隆起的造型使得它成为世界上最容易辨认的飞机。经过特殊设计的这一层，一方面可以用来做头等舱休息室或者用来提供额外的座位，另一方面可以通过移动座椅，安装前货舱门，使飞机很容易地被改装成为货物运输机。这种类型的飞机在正常的布局下可以容纳 366 名乘客。如果改成全经济舱布局，可承载 490 名乘客。该飞机于 1970 年首次用于商业飞行，此后保持载客量记录长达 37 年。波音 747-400 是最常见的，目前仍在服役的飞机类型。其高亚音速的巡航速度可达 570 英里每小时，洲际范围达 7 260 海里。747 飞机上有 6 个厨房、3 个辅助厨房和 12 个厕所。一些航空公司对该飞机内部进行了改装，以便为旅客提供更为奢华和舒适的环境。

除了波音系列，其他常见的美制飞机还有麦道 DC-8、DC-10 以及洛克希德的 Tristar 1011 型等。飞机制造业中的另一个巨头是空客。它是欧洲一家跨国公司。该公司生产并销售了第一架使用数字电传系统的商用客机，如 A320 和 A340。该公司生产的空客 380 是世界上最大的客机。

用于中程和远程飞行的飞机机身主要由两部分构成，飞行员和其他机组人员工作的驾驶舱和供乘客休息的客舱。客舱又可分为前部的头等舱和后部的经济舱。头等舱和经济舱之间有一个舱壁，可以根据每次航班两种客舱的座位数量向前或向后移动。驾驶舱由另一个舱壁与客舱分离。客舱与厨房之间的隔板也叫作舱壁。

除了某些特殊情况，如包机，经济舱的座位数一般会多于头等舱的座位数。头等舱提供高端服务，但通常票价也非常昂贵。头等舱里座椅之间有更大的空间，有些座椅甚至可以变成床铺。另外这里还提供精美的食物和饮品，个性化的服务，等等。经济舱的票价与头等舱相比要便宜得多，因为在这里享受的舒适度较低。座椅之间的距离比较小，食物和娱乐项目的可选择范围也很小。另外飞机上还有商务舱，档次介于这头等舱与经济舱之间。

飞机的载客量取决于运营的航空公司选定的座位布局。如果客舱两边的座位中间只有一个单独的通道，则叫作窄体飞机，例如空客 A320 家族和波音 737。如果座位中间有两条通道，则被称为宽体飞机，例如波音 747 或空客 A380。航空公司通常会发布飞机的座位图供乘客在预定机票或办理登机时选择。上面标示了基本的座位布局、座位号、紧急出口、厕所、厨房、舱壁和机翼的位置。为了记录和方便航班服务组的工作，通常会有一张注明旅客姓名的座位图。机上的座椅都有由数字和字母组成的编号。在一些飞机上，从客舱的左侧开始编以字母“A”，客舱最右侧的座位编以最后一个字母。有时候还会借用最初用于航海的术语“左舷”和“右舷”来分别表示左和右。人们也会用内侧和外侧来表示座椅相对于窗户和过道的位置。内侧表示最靠近过道的座椅，外侧表示最靠近窗户的座椅。中小型飞机的座位号通常从“1”开始，头等舱的 1 号位于飞机前面，经济舱的 1 号位于后面。最大的号码则出现在分隔两个客舱的舱壁处。在头等舱里，有些航空公司还会将乘客的姓名标在座位处。

第二课　超音速飞机

目前所有的民用飞机，包括客机、直升飞机、飞艇，以及许多军用飞机都是亚音速飞机，它们的最大时速小于音速。大多数喷气式飞机以 550 英里/时的亚音速巡航。它们通过空气在前面和后面形成一系列的压力波，类似于船在水中滑行时船头和船尾形成的水波，然而，这种压力波是球形而不是环形的。

在亚音速下，飞机向前方发送相对较小的压力差，作为向前方空气发出的警报信号，因此，空气分子有时间让开并顺畅而平稳地在机翼和尾翼周围流走。

超音速飞行器的飞行速度比音速快，能够达到 1 马赫（在 50 000 英尺高空，1 马赫约等于 660 英里/时），几乎全部用于研究和军事目的。它们以 0.303 英寸（1 英寸=2.54 厘米）口径步枪子弹离膛的初始速度巡航。当飞机接近音速时，前方空气的报警信号变短，使空气分子离开的时间减少，当飞机达到音速时，被压缩的空气分子形成一个更为猛烈的垂直冲击波，冲击波的压力瞬间升高，在声源附近听起来就像鞭子抽打的噼啪声一样。

一旦飞机加速超过 1 马赫，冲击波就会形成一个圆锥体。飞机作为圆锥体的顶点，拖着这个圆锥形的冲击波前进。因为只有在高空才能实现超音速飞行，所以冲击波有足够的时间在到达地面之前扩张。最后，在地面附近，我们听到的冲击波是微弱、低沉的隆隆声。然而，人们仍然担心超音速飞行可能造成的后果，他们抱怨冲击波会损坏人的耳朵和建筑物。事实上，锥体中有两个分别来自机头和机尾的冲击波，这两个冲击波发出两个隆隆声，或是制造持续的空气扰动，听起来就像雷声或远处的爆炸声。

超音速运输机是一种民用的超音速飞行器，旨在用高于音速的速度运送乘客。超音速飞机的机身是流线型的，有尖尖的机头和两个从机头延伸到机尾的薄三角翼。飞机的机头被设计成一个非常锋利的形状，空气在它上面盘旋形成一个强大的涡流，在起飞和降落时增加升力。超音速运输机的窗子设计得较小，以减少气压可能对机舱发生的压迫。

当飞机做跨音速加速时，乘客几乎感觉不到，当飞机在 50 000 英尺的高度以超音速巡航时，向下看地面会感觉它似乎在以正常速度流逝。在超音速飞机上遥望，云彩看来在飞机下面很远的地方，可识别的地面特征非常小。超音速飞机的乘客会看到一幅奇妙的景象：天空看起来像一个深紫色的阴影，地平线显然是弯曲的。

到目前为止，可用于定期航行的超音速客机只有协和飞机和图波列夫 Tu-144 飞机。Tu-144 最后一次载客飞行是在 1978 年 6 月，它的最后一次飞行是在 1999 年美国国家航空航天局的一次飞行中。协和号的最后一次商业飞行是在 2003 年 10 月，2003 年 11 月 26 日的渡轮飞行是其最后一次空降作战。在协和飞机永久停飞之后，再没有用于商业用途的超音速飞机了。最近一些公司提出了一种超音速商用喷气式客机，这可能会使超音速运输方式再次走回人们的视线。

第三课　驾　驶　舱

驾驶舱内一片寂静。只能勉强听到发动机的声音，飞机移动的感觉大部分来自机头周围的空气声。在云层上面，视野开阔，尤其在飞机向着太阳飞行时，令人眼花缭乱。在高空中，其他飞机很难将平流层的明亮光线和深蓝色区分开来。

驾驶舱是根据两位驾驶员不挪动座位就能接触所有的主要操纵器和开关而设计的。驾驶舱内可能有超过 150 个仪表，有些仪表带有数字式读数，大多数仪表带有人们熟悉的圆形刻度盘，但这些仪表并不需要同时注视。驾驶员很少集中注意力于某一仪表，而是不时对全部仪表进行扫视。在每个驾驶员的面前是“基本仪表的 T 形配置”，也就是指示速度、高度、姿态和航向四个主要读数的航空仪表的标准配置。这些仪表之所以这样配置是为了使最重要的仪表最靠近驾驶员。

航空有它自己的传统。因为早期受到陆路和海路靠右行驶规则的影响，飞机在航路上也是靠右飞行。为了便于观察，机长选择坐在左座上。

所有的主要仪表和操作器都是双套的，有的甚至有第三套备用仪表。万一有驾驶员丧失工作能力，另一个驾驶员也有安全飞行所必要的全套操纵器。飞行中，每个驾驶员都可以监视另一驾驶员的仪表，以确保两块仪表板上的仪表给出同样的显示。

主仪表板上还有一个高度复杂的中央警报系统。伴以能够发出响亮嗡嗡声的红色或黄色方形灯能立刻指示出飞机任何一部分及其控制系统发生的故障。18 种不同报警信号中的任何一种刺耳声都能扰乱驾驶舱的宁静。

所有的航空公司可能会很快采用目前只在某些民航班机和军用飞机上使用的装置——电子平视显示器。它把高度、速度、航向和跑道图像用电子方法投射在风挡玻璃上，从而驾驶员在着陆时能“平视地”看到一幅与真跑道结合的图像。这种系统可节约驾驶员将目光从对准仪表调到对准跑道时所失去的极为重要的两三秒时间。

第四课 飞 机 客 舱

影响航空公司收益的一个重要因素就是客舱布局。飞机运载越多的旅客，航空公司获得的利润就越多。如果客舱内座椅配备的空间越大，飞机票也就越贵。因此，飞机设计者在设计客舱布局时要综合考虑各种因素。他们要尽量安排最多的座椅同时保证乘客的舒适度和安全。

在商业载人飞机发展的初期，飞机仅能容纳少量的乘客。例如，福克 F.II 封闭的客舱空间里仅能容纳四名乘客，在开放空间的驾驶舱里，驾驶员旁边有第五个座椅，这个座椅最初是为机械维修师或领航员准备的。福克 F.III 是生产于 20 世纪 20 年代的单引擎高翼单翼飞机。这架飞机仅能装载 5 名乘客。福克 F.XII 是一架由荷兰皇家航空公司订购的三引擎高翼单翼飞机。1931 年，这架飞机开始从阿姆斯特丹至巴达维亚飞行时，机上只能承载 16 名乘客。随着民航技术的革新，座椅一排排不断增多，座椅旁侧也开始出现了过道。

随着飞机开始进行远程飞行，许多飞机配备了卧舱，方便旅客休息。例如，1956 年道格拉斯 DC-7 首航横越大西洋直飞定期航班时，全程大约需要 10 个小时。因此，为了满足乘客对于睡眠的需求，飞机上安装了躺椅式座椅和睡铺。而这些设施随着更快的喷气式飞机的出现而不再被需要了。

高密度座椅配置所带来的潜在经济效益是客舱布局设计的一个重要考虑因素。经典的客舱布局是一排座椅中间配有一条通道。飞机机身的宽度决定了并排座椅的数量。在一些小型飞机上，如比奇 1900，中间通道两侧各有一列单独的座椅。空客 A320 系列，波音 727 和 737 飞机上一排共 6 个座椅，构成了 3+3 的布局模式。机上也有非对称的结构，如 ERJ 系列和 CRJ 系列飞机配置 1+2 的座椅布局模式，道格拉斯 DC9 和 MD80 飞机则是 2+3 的布局模式。一些宽体客机上每排都有更多的座椅，并在座椅中间设计了两个供旅客通行的过道。一些机体更宽的飞机，如波音 747 或空客 380，客舱内每排有 10 个座椅，通常设计为 3+4+3 的模式。

一些商业飞行，为满足乘客不同的需求，客舱被设计分为头等舱、商务舱和经济舱。有些飞机，如往来两地的班机、穿梭飞机、包机等只有单一等级的客舱。从不同的座位布局中即可看出明显的差别。

第五课 客 舱 服 务

经过几十年的发展，客舱服务和最初相比已大不相同。第一批航空公司在准确自我定位之前一直仿效豪华巨型远洋客轮上的那种宫殿式豪华。在 20 世纪 30 年代，在优雅的飞艇和精致的飞行船上，乘客可以在华丽的餐厅里悠闲用餐，享受厨师和服务员提供的美食。

然而，大规模的旅行和对速度的要求忽略了对舒适度的追求，需要大量的食品和饮料供应。大航空公司如新加坡航空公司每年要提供超过 1 800 万份的航空餐食，投资大约 5 亿美元在客舱服务上。基本上，机上餐食是在大型的餐饮中心配制的，这些餐饮中心通常是在航线两头的当地机场租用的。为了保证餐食的味道和口感，餐食供应可能由大饭店、餐馆或专业公司承包。餐食必须在飞机起飞前 20～40 分钟运上飞机，通常是凉菜和随时可以在飞机上加热的饭菜。一些食物，如预烤牛排，需要在由飞机引擎供电的烤箱里烘烤。事实上，并不是所有的机场都有足够的食物供应设施，所以冷冻食品已经成为航班必需品。冷冻食品需要加热 30 秒钟才能在烤箱中融化。从某种意义上说，新鲜食品提高了航空餐食的水准，但它不能长期保存。一旦遇到航班延误，新鲜食品很可能会变质。因为在加压舱里的牛奶很快就会变酸，而且在某些地方牛奶也不是随时都买到，所以一些航空公司用奶粉代替新鲜牛奶。

精致的餐食是飞行中不可缺少的一部分，特别是对于头等舱和商务舱的旅客来说。越来越多的航空公司开始与米其林厨师合作，并努力设计各种菜单。如新加坡航空公司投资了 3 000 万美元开发一种新型的机上厨房。

餐食的种类取决于不同的航空公司和不同的旅行舱位。餐食可以放在托盘里或者由很多道菜组成，不用托盘，搭配桌布、金属餐具、玻璃器皿（一般在头等舱和商务舱）。食物常常反映航空公司所在国家的文化。厌倦了国际流行的烤鸡和牛排，旅客有时会对民族菜肴表达出浓厚的兴趣：大多数东方国家的航空公司提供了可供选择的民族菜肴菜单。

航空公司的正餐通常包括肉（最常见的是鸡肉或牛肉）、鱼或面食；沙拉或蔬菜；小面包卷和甜点。调味品（通常是盐、胡椒粉和糖）用小袋或小瓶包装。配餐公司也可以为限制性饮食的旅客提供特殊膳食，这些通常必须提前订购，一般在购票时提出。一些常见的特殊餐食的例子包括：

- 文化类餐食，如土耳其餐、法国餐、意大利餐、中餐、韩餐、日餐或印度餐等。
- 婴儿餐，一些航空公司也提供儿童餐，包括孩子们喜欢的食物，如烘焙的豆子、迷你汉堡和热狗等。
- 医疗餐，包括低/高纤维餐、低脂肪/胆固醇餐、糖尿病餐、无花生餐、无乳糖餐、低盐/钠餐、低嘌呤餐、低卡路里餐、低蛋白餐、清淡（非辛辣）餐和无麸质膳食餐等。
- 宗教餐，包括犹太教餐、清教徒餐、印度教餐、佛教餐和耆那教素食者（有时称为亚洲素食者）餐等。
- 素食餐，一些航空公司不提供非严格素食者的特殊素餐食，相反，旅客会得到严格素食餐。

在亚洲全业务航空公司的航班上和几乎所有长途航班上，食物通常是免费的，但在低成本的航空公司或欧洲全业务航空公司的航班上食物可能需要额外支付费用。食物的品质通常取决于航空公司的经济状况。中国国际航空公司的报告说，国内航班的每餐需要 50 元人民币（7.30 美元），而国际航班需要 70 元人民币（10 美元）。然而，这个数字在不同的航空公司是有区别的，有些航空公司报告的每餐成本只有 3.50 美元。

机组人员的餐食菜单更加多样化。为了避免同时食物中毒，机长和副机长通常吃不同的食物，并且禁止食用贝类。

进餐时间随起飞时间而定，并使用国际标准时间。遇有颠簸情况，进餐时间会有所调整。合理安排加热和供应的时间，不让旅客吃不冷不热的食物。

每天到达停机坪的第一辆服务车通常是伙食供应车。供应餐食的职工把脏的器皿和废物搬走，将新的装上飞机。据说英国航空公司每周要处理大约 50 万套餐具、16.8 万只玻璃杯、5 万张盘子、4 万套杯碟，清理大约 100 吨亚麻餐布和毛毯。这可真是一个大工程。

第六课　空中领航（I）

驾驶员要能在空中找到所飞的航路，就必须知道自己的位置和方向。使用简单的磁罗盘定向是容易的，每个驾驶舱内至少有一套这种设备。另一种飞机罗盘使用陀螺仪。现代的飞机罗盘是复杂而高效率的。驾驶员定位要比定向困难，需要一些复杂的设备。

如果驾驶员只会用罗盘、地图和目视指示器进行领航，空中旅行就总是会受到限制。飞机上装备的无线电设备定位相当于海员用灯塔定位。其优点是：无线电不需看到即可见效。用于远程导航的无线电长波沿着地球表面曲线传播，直线传播的无线电短波则用于短程导航系统。

但是即便是最复杂的无线电导航系统也和将头探出驾驶舱去测定某个教堂或河流的目视方位这种简单的方法有共同之处：即二者都依靠地面辅助设备。多普勒雷达和气象雷达等最新装置则完全不需要辅助设备。惯性制导系统也是如此，它的精确测量装置能将飞机的轻微加速度记录下来。

在未来的年代里，这些导航系统将由非常低频的奥米伽无线电台网，激光设备和卫星系统加以完善。

推测领航（有时叫作“ded”——推论的航迹计算）。轻型飞机的驾驶员仍在沿用这种最古老最简单的空中领航方法。这种领航方法依赖于地面上可以识别的标志。驾驶员起飞前在地图上标出航迹，依靠罗盘保持正确的航向。驾驶员知道了飞行的速度就能计算何时该飞越某个地标，并以此来校对他的进程。

风使飞机偏离航线或造成飞机突然加速或减速，打乱了这种简单的领航。把最后一个已知位置和飞行方向及速度联系起来，驾驶员就能在飞行中多次确定自己的近似位置。这近似位置就成为所谓误差圆圈的中心。该圆圈的半径约等于从最后一个地标算起的已飞距离的 10%。

第七课　空中领航（II）

无线电导航广泛应用于商业飞行中。飞行员通过调节机载无线电导航设备接收地面导航台发射的信号。依据这个信号，飞行员不仅能够知道飞机是向台还是背台，也能够了解飞机是否偏离航线，从而对航向进行相应的修正。

伏尔（VOR）是最常见的一种导航系统。它提供了向台和背台的磁方位信息。如果与测距器（DME）联合使用，这种助航设备称为伏尔/测距器（VOR/DME）系统。如果伏尔与军用塔康（TACAN）导航设备合用，该设备称为伏塔克（VORTAC）。在这些设备出现以前，空中导航主要依赖于与无方向性信标（NDB）一起工作的无线电罗盘低频接收机。

低频无线电接收机发射的信号指引飞行员向台归航，然后飞行员依据一定的程序又可以飞离该台。然而，这些无方向信标易受到气象以及其他因素的干扰，例如衰弱的信号，其他导航台的干扰等。而这些干扰可能会造成机载仪表的故障。

惯性导航系统（INS）、远距离无线电导航系统（Loran）和台卡导航系统（Decca）是民航系统中常用的三种跨洋导航系统。

惯性导航系统（INS）是一种自主导航系统，一旦启动该系统不依赖于外界就可以确定自身位置、方向或速度。因而这种系统不会受到外界干扰，适用于远距离飞越水域或大陆而无须足够的地面无线电台导航的飞行。

远距离无线电导航系统（Loran）是一种双曲线无线电导航系统，由美国在二战期间研发。与旧系统相比，该系统提供更远的航程，精确性也更高。太平洋水域广阔，且缺少有用的导航点，因此，太平洋战争期间远距离无线电导航系统以其优势广泛应用于海洋与空中导航。后来又研发了改良版的性能更优越的远距离无线电-C 系统（原来的则被叫作远距离无线电-A 系统），并逐渐取代了以前的导航系统。

与远距离无线电导航系统一样，台卡（Decca）也是一种双曲线无线电导航系统。船只或飞机通过接收到的由固定的导航台发出的无线电信号来确定自身位置。该系统的精确性要优于罗兰系统。这种导航系统是由英国研发并首次在二战中被英国皇家海军所使用。使用远距离无线电导航系统或台卡导航系统的飞机要有接收特殊信号的设备，这些信号从发射台不断发出，指出飞机精确的位置。

自 20 世纪 60 年代以来，卫星导航系统逐步应用于导航领域。其中一种就是全球定位系统（GPS），这是一种基于太空的无线电导航系统。其精确性要比以往任何陆基导航系统都更高。并且可以应用于地球上任何位置。该系统只需依赖几颗卫星即可覆盖全球。其独特优势已经引起了全球关注，这种导航系统拥有广阔的应用前景。

第八课　空中交通管制

在浩瀚无垠的天空中，飞机似乎可以不受约束地随意飞行，想往哪飞就往哪飞，其实并非如此。就像车辆在地面行驶必须遵守交通规则、接受警察的指挥一样，飞机在天上飞行也必须要遵守空中交通规则，受到专业人员的指挥与调度。空中交通管制员就是专业人员，他们必须保证飞机在机场周围上空的分离，让飞机可以从不同方向，以不同的速度飞行，并在不同高度上相互飞越。

空中交通管制是由地面空中交通管制员提供的一种服务，它指挥地面上的飞机以及经过控制空域的飞机，并为非控制空域中的飞机提供咨询服务。在许多国家，空中交通管制为所有在其领空内运行的私用、军用和商用飞机提供服务。根据航班类型和空域类别，空中交通管制员发出飞行员必须执行的指令，或者给出建议（在一些国家被称为“飞行信息”），飞行员酌情采纳或忽略。

两架飞机之间的起飞时间间隔受到严格管制。同一类型的飞机，起飞方向不同，它们之间的最小时间间隔通常是一分钟，然而，如果它们向同一方向起飞，时间间隔就是两分钟。由于宽体客机起飞时会产生尾部气流，后面起飞的轻型飞机通常要晚起飞 10 分钟来避开气流。当飞机已经安全分离并按照标准仪表起飞程序飞离机场以后，空中交通管制员就把它移交给第一雷达扇形区管制员，由他发布爬升到巡航高度的许可。

飞机通常沿着航路飞行，航路划分为三个主要高度层。从45 000英尺到75 000英尺（可使用的空域限制）是超音速和高空飞行飞机使用的最高高度；低于最高高度的是亚音速喷气机使用的较低的航路；再下面的高度通常是由较慢的涡轮螺旋桨飞机和由螺旋桨驱动的飞机使用的航路。由于许多空域被严格用于军事目的，民用航线通常是在军用空域之间的狭小空隙中开辟的。

在世界范围内的空中交通管制系统中，空中交通管制员担负着保障空中交通安全、有序、快速、高效运行的职责。他们通常驻守在空中交通管制中心和地面控制塔上，通过雷达和视觉雷达监视飞机在指定的空域内的位置、速度和高度，并通过无线电向飞行员发出指令。

在大多数国家，驻扎在空中交通管制中心的空管人员被称为"区域""进近"或者按照美国的叫法，"中心"管制员。区域管制员负责飞机在繁忙机场和空域的较高海拔高度的安全，区域管制员也负责飞机在较低的高度以及没有自己的塔台或进近控制器的小机场周围的空中交通安全。

机场或塔台管制员控制机场附近的飞机，并使用机场塔楼进行目视观测。塔台管控的空域范围是机场周围5海里（9.3千米）半径，空域大小和形状取决于交通配置与容量。塔台岗位被划分为很多种，例如飞行数据/放行许可、地面管制、本地管制（被飞行员称为"塔台"）；在繁忙的设施中，还需要有限的雷达进场控制。

空中交通管制员的岗位要求具有高度专业化的知识、技能和能力。分工不同的管制员运用分离规则保持飞机之间的安全距离，并指挥所有飞机安全而有效率地通过指定的领空区域以及地面。因为管制员在值班时肩负着巨大的责任（通常是在航空上，"在岗位上"），并且每天都要做出无数的实时决策，所以这个职业一直被认为是世界上最具挑战性的职业之一，又因为需要时刻面临许多变数（如设备、配置、天气、交通量、人的因素等），其压力之大可想而知。然而，许多管制员认为这份工作最大的优点是高薪水和极大的、说一不二的自主权。

通信是空中交通管制工作的一个相当重要的部分：管制员要能准确捕捉飞行员和其他管制员说的话，因为仅对飞行高度和跑道号码的一个误解，就有可能酿成灾难性的后果。管制员通过即按即说对讲系统与飞行员联络，这种系统伴随许多问题，如一次只能在一个频率上进行一次传输，并且可能会混淆沟通双方得到的信息，使其变得难以理解。

尽管空中交通管制员在通信时使用本地语言，但全世界航空的默认语言是英语。那些英语不是第一语言的管制员通常需要掌握最低限度水平的英语语言能力。

团队合作在管制员的工作中起着重要的作用，不仅需要与其他的管制员和空中交通工作人员协作，还要与飞行员、工程师和管理者配合。

第九课　管 制 塔 台

管制塔台是机场的枢纽中心。在最繁忙的国际空港中心，管制员一天可指挥多达2 000

架次飞机的起飞和着陆。在高峰期间每分钟要指挥一架飞机。

塔台必须相当的高，以便于管制员能够对整个机场一览无遗。在一所俱乐部的机场内，塔台可能只是一间双层小屋，一个管制员从这里指挥飞机在一条简易跑道上起落。或者像戴高乐机场那样用整块石料建筑起的高达 260 英尺的管制台，有七人或更多人一组的管制员来观察方圆 11 平方英里的复杂跑道网。

大型机场的管制塔台有两间管制室。在顶层的目视管制室内的管制员负责飞机的起飞、滑行和最后的着陆指示。助理员记录飞机的起飞和到达时间，从而为收取着陆费做准备，用计算机打印出每架飞机的预计到达时间和规定的起飞时间。地面动态计划管制员为离场飞机预定航路上的位置（可用时间）。

在灯光暗淡的进近管制室中笼罩着一种沉着的紧迫气氛。进近管制室通常位于下层。这里，在雷达荧光屏的橙黄色灯光中工作的进近管制员把进场的飞机引进跑道。如因检查跑道或风向转变而改变着陆方向，或在高峰期间跑道超载等造成延误，就将飞机安排在分层盘旋等待区。围绕无线电信标台飞行，直到发给着陆许可。进近管制员综合二层或更多层飞机，移交给雷达指挥员。雷达指挥员按进场航道把飞机拉开，排成一条单行。进港航班三到四英里的安全间隔距离提供了大约一分钟的降落间隔。飞越拥挤机场区的飞机由另一名雷达指挥员管制。

雷达荧光屏上有若干同心的圆周，叫作距离标志。它表示离天线有 2 英里、5 英里或 10 英里的距离。借助于雷达荧光屏上叠加的一个方向刻度盘，管制员就能准确地计算出飞机的位置。虚线和实线环绕无线电导航参考点。尖头信号或目标信号指出每架移动的飞机。在现代的字母数字式显示器中，每个目标信号都标有航班号，飞机的高度和航线，以便快速地识别。尖头信号会不断衰减，然后随着新位置的出现而增加亮度。

在小区域内跟踪迅速移动的数十架飞机，要求管制员精神高度集中。管制员在雷达荧光屏前最多工作两小时，就该松弛一下，休息 30 分钟。

第十课　飞 行 计 划

在每架飞机起飞前，飞行员或飞行签派人员需要向当地的民航当局申报飞行计划。飞行计划是非常重要的文件，它指明了飞机计划的飞行路线。过去老式的飞行计划室里飞行员在长桌前研究航图和其他文件的情况如今已经被装有各种电子设备的现代办公室所取代，航班通常会在不到半小时内签派。

飞行机组在飞行前一小时左右办理相关手续。有些航空公司的机组人员由于经常在一起工作，彼此非常了解，因此会结成小组一起工作。而有些时候，机组人员可能甚至都没有见过面。如果有任何机组人员因故缺席，就会让替补人员接手。

将一些关键信息，如飞机信息，出发地和目的地，旅客、货物、行李和燃油等，航路上以及目的地最新的天气变化等，输入电脑中就会得到一些可能的优化路线（最小距离、最短时间、最低成本）。然后选出最佳路线。如果几个飞行机组想要同一路线，通常会按照先到先得的方式进行分配。

飞机会按照规定的航路飞行。航路可以被看作是一个针对飞机的三维高速公路。但它们不一定连接两座城市。飞机会沿着由导航台发出的无线电波飞行。大多数航路宽 8 海里（12.87 千米），航路高度在垂直方向上可让上下飞机达到至少 1 000 英尺的距离。航路通常在导航台处分开，这里规定了一个航路与另一航路的交叉点。航路的名称由一个或多个字母加上一个和多个数字组成，如 R342 或 G17。飞行员由一个导航台飞向另一个导航台，但有时也会因为航路上的恶劣天气而选择绕飞。

计划远程飞行时飞行员可采用大圆航线，这是起飞点和终点之间的最短距离。尤其当两点之间没有航路连接时。尽管这种航线飞起来较困难，但是现代的导航技术使得这种方式变为可能。

燃油的计算是飞行计划中影响安全的最重要方面。这种计算有点儿复杂，因为在计算时必须要综合考虑各种因素，如路线的选择、天气预报、飞机重量等。通常来说，飞机越重，耗油率会越高。由于燃油本身也是飞机总重的一部分，因此载油的同时也会耗油。除了要带足到达目的地的燃油外，飞机还要携带遇到紧急状况时所需的燃油，如改航、等待、逆风等情况，以保证飞行安全。每次飞行前都装载最大油量是很不明智的，尤其当飞行距离较短或者当飞机在短跑道上起飞或着陆时。然而，由于各地油价不同，为避免在油价高的地方加油，选择在油价便宜的地方加满油并在航路上消耗多余的燃油也是合理的。

导航和天气数据表，目的地机场以及备降场的相关信息，重要人士以及商业重要人士的名单，乘客特殊需求的信息以及飞行计划构成了一大堆的文件。机长在上面签字同意并由签派人员确认。最后连同紧急设备和程序的清单一起呈递至国家空中交通管制服务单位。副本则用电传分发至沿航路的各管制中心。带着这些得到授权的数据资料，飞行机组准备登机。

第十一课　天 气 预 报

每个航班的平稳安全运行都离不开机场气象部门提供的详细气象数据。每天在黎明前，值班预报员就已进入一个高度紧张的状态，他们从陆地、海洋、外层空间的气象站以及飞行中的飞行员那里收集通宵传来的天气数据并进行研究。计算机将它们完全消化后，天气数据以代码的形式通报给飞行员，给出尽可能详细的信息，以便飞行员根据航空条例来确定天气是否适合飞行。

航空公司的飞行员必须在起飞前了解预期的起飞条件。雾现在已经成为导致令人厌烦的飞机延误的罪魁祸首。当雾在机场上空弥漫在 1 000 英尺以上时，尤其令飞行员恼火。飞行员需要了解天气什么时候放晴，雾是否还会重来？当潮湿空气做水平运动，经过寒冷的表面被冷却液化时，雾常常发生。当暖锋经过积雪覆盖区域时，雾也很普遍。雾在海上最常见，当潮湿空气遇到较冷的海水，包括冷水上升区域时，常常出现雾。在水面或空地上有足够强的温差也会引起雾。结冰发生在稍低于冰点的潮湿空气中，飞机在起飞时用喷气发动机的热气给机翼除冰，这将减少起飞马力，因此可能需要调整载重。

航空公司的飞行员需要了解飞行时间在 30 分钟内的各个机场的地面情况。如果起飞后发动机失灵，飞行员可能需要找一个本地的备降机场。机场候机楼天气预报（TAFs）是大型机场天气事务处的气象专家做出的，他们对本港的天气模式非常了解。

天气预报员整天绘制天气图，并不断更新。天气图给出了地面的一般天气以及高海拔地区的天气图，通过这些天气图，飞行员可以得到强低压和周围大风的预警。在低压区的一边，飞机会遇到顶风，要使用较多燃油，但在另一边，顺风却缩短了飞行时间，减少了燃油消耗。急流是一种非常强的风，吹向地球大气层，对天气有重要的影响。气象学家利用一些急流的位置作为天气预报的辅助工具。急流与商业的相关性主要体现在航空飞行中，因为飞行时间会显著地受到顺流或逆流飞行的影响，会在很大程度上影响航空公司的燃料和时间成本。航空公司常常因为这个原因随急流而飞。动态的北大西洋航迹是航空公司和空中交通管制员齐心协力适应急流和高空风的一个例子，这会给航空公司和其他用户带来最大利益。

重要天气预报是飞机燃油计算的重要参考之一。这些天气预报会提醒飞行员注意雷暴天气，雷暴天气通常伴随着强风、大雨，有时还有雪、雨夹雪、冰雹，或者恰恰相反，一点降水都没有。雷暴是由于温暖潮湿的空气迅速向上运动造成的，有时是沿着一个锋面。当雷暴在终点机场隆隆作响时，飞机不得不在巨大的雷雨湍流和锋利的风切变中降落。不利的风切变可能会使飞机的速度降低 60 英里/小时以上，因此天气预报员必须密切关注。

有时，即使在晴朗的天空中，飞机也可能会遇到一种特殊的鹅卵石式的颠簸。晴空湍流是气团在没有任何诸如云之类的可视线索的情况下发生的湍流运动，是由以不同速度运动的气团相遇所引起的。严重的晴空湍流能使飞机发生明显摇动，甚至改变飞行高度，但是，如果飞行员能改变飞行高度层，摇动的时间不会持续很久。2017 年 5 月 1 日，一架航班号是 SU270 的波音 777 飞机在从莫斯科飞往泰国的途中遭遇晴空湍流，飞机突然下降，机上 27 名乘客因未扣好安全带而受重伤。飞行员稳定住飞机继续飞行，所有需要医疗照顾的旅客到达后被送往曼谷医院。

飞行中，机组需要收听连续不断的甚高频空中天气预报，监视飞机的气象雷达。万一遇到暴风雨，他们必须尽力飞越或绕过它。风暴中的闪电不会对飞机造成结构损坏，但它可以烧毁天线或干扰无线电导航设备，特别是在较低的高度。冰雹是对飞机伤害最严重的灾害之一。当冰雹直径超过 0.5 英寸（13 毫米）时，飞机会在几秒内受到严重损坏。机组也要为预防风切变而监视惯性导航设备。

天气无国界。面对各种天气信息和数据，航空公司飞行员不必为翻译困难而担忧，因为气象学家已经开发了一种全球通用的气象语言。

第十二课 紧急情况

事故确实会发生。事故发生时，机组训练的情况，机载设备以及旅客的良好常识是幸存的根本条件。对发生紧急情况的可能性要警惕（但不要过分担心）才能增加幸存的机会。

飞机座椅上的安全带和座椅一样，是设计来抵御飞机的突然减速的。要学会怎样很快系上和松开安全带。客舱乘务人员在飞机起飞和着陆时要检查安全带是否系好，婴儿是否安置在特制的儿童小床上。

切勿忽视飞行开始时的安全示范表演，除非你对这些事情已很熟练。学好怎样穿救生衣和怎样使用放在座位上面或前座靠背上的紧急氧气面罩：如果在高空突然发生机舱失压，就没有时间想怎样戴面罩了。每个杂志袋内有张带图的安全说明卡。它指出紧急出口的位置。每个出口有以一种或几种文字说明操作的指示牌，以便旅客可以开门。

灭火器和消防斧存放在乘务组那里。救生艇通常存放在每个主要出口附近；在宽机身喷气机上，救生艇是逃生滑梯的延伸，在 VC10、707 和 747 之类的飞机内，这些东西存放在通道上面的舱壁内。救生箱，急救箱和极地箱通常放在救生艇或出口处附近，也许固定在救生艇上或出口处。

如果在飞行中亮出“系上安全带”的信号，应该立刻听从；飞机可能即将进入颠簸的气流之中，四处走动的乘客，尤其是后排的乘客可能会被抛扔起来。

“请勿抽烟”的信号一亮，要立即把香烟熄灭（在烟盘内，切勿丢在地板上）。在使用易燃材料做装饰品的厕所内要绝对禁止抽烟。1946—1976 年，有 316 起事故是由于机内着火或冒烟引起的：而很多是从厕所开始的。

在发生紧急情况时，要毫无疑问地听从乘务人员的指挥。他们会指示乘客系上安全带，熄灭烟头，支撑自己的身体以防突然减速（支撑身体的位形在安全说明卡上有图示）。当飞机停下来时，他们操纵出口，告诉旅客撤离程序并收集紧急设备和供应品。如果舱门打不开，他们就起动紧急出口，同时叫乘客松开安全带，留下所有的东西，按乘务人员的指示走向指定的滑梯。

在舱门口，跳下或滑下滑梯到地面上（或进入救生艇）。然后远离飞机。行动要快，要忘掉随身行李。着火时，掉队的人可能会被燃烧着的客舱设备所释放出来的有毒气体熏倒。

第十三课　维护与维修

飞机维护指的是对于飞机或飞机零部件进行彻底检修，修理，检查或改善。飞机维护是航空业必不可少的一部分，它有助于保持飞机良好的性能，提高使用率，确保飞行安全。飞机维护是最重要的飞行前活动。

在人类首次尝试飞机飞行时可能就已经有了飞机维护与维修。当时的飞机还只是由棉质物覆盖的木质结构的机器。这些木质的机器由于其结构脆弱，因此在维修的过程中很容易受损。随着时间的推进，技术的进步推动飞机维修更加精密系统，以应付飞机的复杂结构。飞机维护的任务，参与人员以及检查步骤都有着严格的规定。专业的维修技师要经过培训并获得当地航空当局颁发的资质才能上岗维修飞机的机身、发动机和各个系统。

对飞机各个装置进行令人满意的维修是飞机制造商的职责。为了使潜在顾客相信一架新飞机的安全性，他们必须获得相关机构颁发的适航证书。他们还要编写维修手册和服务通告来说明飞机及零部件的维护与维修，并根据操纵飞机的飞行员的反馈不断更新这些数据。

维修日程规定了飞机每一部分要接受检查的时间，检查的类型和程度以及依据飞行小时数、着陆次数和其他标准对某些零部件进行的更换。航空公司须将这些资料呈递给适航当局以便维持其维修团队。为了获得批准，还需要满足一些基本的要求，包括提供合适的机库和车间，必要的工具和设施，质量和可靠性管理，完备的培训体系和设备等。

机库要足以容纳宽飞机的机身。在机库里，飞机周围建造了巨大的检修架，上面配备了多层工作平台、灯光设施、升降机和传送带，这样机务维修人员便可以对飞机每一部分进行彻底详细的检查和修理。

不同飞机有不同的维修要求。飞机每一部分需要进行维护的时间间隔也不同。例如，发动机通常每隔 500 飞行小时进行检查，客舱窗户以及机身上其他开口处大约每隔 300 飞行小时进行检查。通常说来，飞机有 50～60 飞行小时的小型检修，300～600 小时的过夜检修，每飞行 3 600 小时的全面检修。

第十四课　机　　场

世界上的大型机场被设计得如同设施齐备的城市。它们是航空运输和各种地面运输的交汇点，可以满足旅客、工作人员、迎宾员以及其他现代航空运输体验者的各种需求。由于靠得很近，机场还与当地居民区和近郊区有密切的关系。

最早的飞机起飞和着陆的地点是在草坪上。飞机可以选取有利风向，从任何角度着陆。后来做了小提升，将草坪改为土道，消除了草的阻力。然而，土道的飞机场只有在干燥条件下才好用。后来，混凝土跑道使飞机着陆不再受任何气象条件的限制。

飞机噪声是对机场附近居民造成干扰的主要原因。如果机场夜间和清晨运营，附近居民的睡眠会受到影响。飞机噪声不仅来自于飞机的起飞和着陆，还包括飞机维护和测试等地面操作。噪声会对人们的健康造成影响。其他伴随的噪声和环境问题来自于去机场途中的车辆拥堵所造成的噪声和污染。因为新建机场或对现有机场增加跑道都会对农村、历史遗迹、当地植物群和动物群造成影响，所以往往受到当地居民的抵制。由于鸟类和飞机之间存在碰撞风险，大型机场采取鸟群数量控制项目，对鸟类进行恐吓和射杀。机场建设已经改变了当地的天气模式。例如，因为他们经常把大片地区夷为平地，所以导致以前很少形成雾的地方也出现了雾。此外，它们通常变草木为路面，还会改变农业区的排水方式，导致周围的土地发生更多的洪水、径流和侵蚀。随着科技的发展，机场建设已成为一把双刃剑。

幸运的是，机场建设正朝着更好的方向发展。飞机的设计和制造更多地关注较大尺寸和较少噪声，大型飞机减少了起落次数的增长率。随着大型机场逐渐成为贸易、旅游和就业的中心，它们正在稳步转变为当地居民区的“好邻居”。

现代机场必须尽可能地与当地居民和谐相处，同时还要关注航空旅客、航空公司及其员工的利益。安全、方便、飞行正常是当局计划和运营机场时必须考虑的三个要素。机场必须坐落在进近和起飞航道中没有障碍物和危险物的地方，跑道要有适当的长度和强度，装有适当的灯光与必不可少的无线电和雷达设备，滑行道要有适当的宽度并能引导至靠近候机楼的宽阔的停机坪。

在过去的许多年里，机场建设一直致力于建造更长、更坚固的跑道，以满足更大和更快的飞机需求。然而，现代技术正开始致力于缩短距离。在遥远的将来，一条 12 000 英尺长的跑道也足以满足载重多达 500 吨且速度最快的超音速喷气机使用，即使是在大热天发动机功率降低时。唯一的例外是海拔较高的机场，由于空气稀薄，那就要大大地增加起飞和着陆的安全距离。

越来越多的人使用机场，当局已尽一切努力满足人们对舒适和方便的要求。他们尽可能地缩短从到达点到飞机的步行距离。当局的目标是要保证进、出机场的最佳通路，不但可经公路和铁路，也可经地下铁道和直升机；他们提供足够的停车位，建造明确的路标和设施齐全的候机大楼。虽然很少有机场能够完全满足这些要求，但在现代化和扩张的平稳过程中，大家都在努力实现这一目标。

大多数机场的名称包含地点。许多机场还以公众人物的名字命名，通常有政治家（如夏尔·戴高乐国际机场）、君王（如贾特拉帕蒂·希瓦吉国际机场）、文化领袖（如利物浦约翰·列侬机场），或航空史上的一位杰出人物（如悉尼的金斯福德·史密斯国际机场），有时甚至是著名的诗人（例如阿拉马·伊克巴勒国际机场）。一些机场还有非官方的名字，并且可能广泛流传以至于它的官方名称很少被人知晓。一些机场名称包括“国际”一词，表示它们有处理国际空中交通的能力，这包括一些没有规划国际航空服务的机场（例如奥尔巴尼国际机场）。

第十五课　机场消防队

全部飞机事故中有 75%发生在离机场半英里以内。飞机失火很少见——伦敦希思罗机场 1977 年发生过两起——但是机场如果没有高效的消防措施是不准营业的。

机场的消防队遇到着陆的飞机稍不正常时（如轮胎憋气，任一重要系统的自动保险电门断开，驾驶舱的一个警告灯发亮），就要出动，准备进行全面的应急行动。大机场的消防队平均每天出动一次，而且在坏天气和有雾时总是常备不懈。在紧急情况下，消防队提供全部紧急援助，载运担架并帮助丧失行动能力的人。

飞机燃烧很快，消防人员要在三分钟以内到达出事地点，进行灭火和救援工作。直到 20 世纪 60 年代，机场的灭火设备仅有改装的城市消防队所用的灭火设备。现在每个大机场都配有快速介入车（RIV），警报后两分钟就能抵达跑道。重型功能车辆的设计目的是穿越崎岖不平的地面，到达远处的跑道（通过迂回的路线，它们不能在使用中的跑道上行驶），或者到达最容易发生事故的目测高接和低接地区。

除非符合那些根据国际民航组织的建议而制定的国家标准，否则，一律不给机场颁发执照，但各机场可以根据自己的需要进行装备。印度有些机场备有坦克履带补给车，新西兰奥克兰机场在退潮时使用气垫船来通过泥洼地。

快速介入车是携带泡沫、水和医疗救护设备并能在大雾与黑暗中使用照明灯的快速卡车。快速介入车的消防人员可以进行抑制火势蔓延的工作和扫清逃生的路线。接着就是重型泡沫消防车，重泡车不但大，而且又快又机动，比快速介入车多带十倍多的泡沫。装在转架上的泡沫枪（“喋喋不休的人”）能旋转喷射泡沫高达 300 英尺。

泡沫熄灭火焰，使周围冷却下来以免死灰复燃。水实际上只能在用作冷却剂时有效。在跑道上撒一层泡沫以防止带故障的飞机在着陆时起火，现在看来是浪费时间，但泡沫对于在加油过程中发生的火灾是有用的，因为燃料箱中积聚的静电会引发燃料火花。煤油比很多航空公司使用的燃油不易燃烧，但价钱较贵。

在轮子、车胎或电气设备局部着火时，粉剂是最有效的，但它一碰到泡沫就产生毒气。如卤代皖 1200 之类的惰性挥发气体能袭击氧气，对发动机起火特别管用。

机场周围各点都驻有紧急消防队。它们相互之间以及它们与中央站和管制塔台之间都有无线电联系。

机场消防人员穿戴防火的铝化衣服，备有防御飞机内家具燃烧时产生的火烟和毒气的呼吸设备。他们每天训练，在机场较远地方的旧机身上操练灭火技巧。

第十六课 机场安检

全世界每天都有大量的人口搭乘飞机旅行。机场上集中的人群使得这里变成各种走私、偷窃、非法移民、恐怖主义以及其他犯罪活动的场所。与机场主候机楼隔开的货运站也常常被盗贼小偷光顾，尤其是在货物装载和运输的过程中。这些非法活动每年都会造成巨大的经济损失。

机场安保工作旨在防止任何威胁或有潜在危险局面的发生，保证旅客、机组人员和飞机的安全，支持国际安全和反恐政策。为了保卫民航业免受非法活动的侵犯，需要采取一系列的先进技术和手段。

恐怖主义是最可怕的威胁。自从 1930 年一架秘鲁航空公司的飞机遭遇劫机，空中的“海盗”行为从未停止过。自 1969 年开始，出现了超过 400 起的劫机事件，其中一半都成功了。因此全世界各个国家开始致力于提高机场和飞行安全。特别自 911 恐怖袭击事件后，国内外航班的安保工作都变得更加严格。面临风险的机场和航空公司会使用 X 射线检查货物，或者像汉莎航空公司的货运站那样，将集装箱的货物减压 12 小时，以避免飞行中货舱发生爆炸。有些货物可能甚至需要放在安全的地方存放超过 24 小时或者需要经过航空当局授权的特殊处理程序进行处置。

旅客们到了航站楼以后也要接受一系列的安检。他们要出示飞机票、登机牌和有效的身份信息，如身份证、护照、士兵证等证件。有些国家还会获取乘客的指纹或者利用视网膜和虹膜扫描来检查人员身份。除此之外，扫描设施还包括手持探测器、金属探测器和全身扫描机器，这种机器实质上是对人进行 X 射线扫描。这些设备用于检测藏匿的随身携带的危险物品，如爆炸物、易燃物、有毒物品、武器等。有些国家不只依赖于这些设备，经过特训的人员还会主动与乘客进行攀谈来探查潜在威胁。通常，完成安检的乘客可以去候机隔离区等待登机，有些从国内航班上下来的乘客也可以待在这里免于再次接受安检。然而，即使如此，必要时这些乘客也要接受随时检查。

由于搜身检查有损尊严，耗时且效率不高，大多数机场使用电磁金属探测器检查乘客。

旅客随身携带的物品，如手提包等通常是用小剂量 X 射线设备进行目视搜查的。在有些机场，还会使用嗅探狗来探测藏匿的危险违禁品。

然而，机场安保工作最终依赖于训练有素的检测设备操作员和经验丰富的安保工作人员。

第十七课　航空公司的正点问题

如果你是一个经验丰富的旅行者，你肯定经历过航班延误的挫败感。精心规划了一个假期或商务旅行后，你提前来到机场，却发现航班要晚点一个小时（或几个小时）。这种情况经常发生。事实上，航班延误现象如此普遍以至于如果一个机场能够保证 80%的航班正点起飞，那么它就可以被大家接受。

对民航旅客的调查显示，几乎所有旅客都认为航空公司的正点问题是航空公司最有价值的组成部分，它已成为影响航空公司产品质量的决定性因素。

航班延误是指航空公司航班起飞或降落晚于预定时间。美国联邦航空管理局（FAA）认为当实际时间比预定时间晚 15 分钟以上时就是航班延误。当航空公司由于某种原因无法运营航班时，还会发生航班取消的情况。

航班延误不仅给航空公司带来了损失，也给旅客带来了损失。在美国，联邦航空管理局估计航空公司每年花在航班延误上的费用达 220 亿美元。当国内航班在停机坪滞留超过 3 小时或国际航班超过 4 小时，航空公司就要被迫向联邦当局支付费用。航班延误给旅客带来不便，如果由于延误而赶不上原计划的活动和会议也将给旅客造成一定的经济损失。那些需要中转的旅客还有可能错过转接班机。遭遇航班延误的旅客常常会伴随愤怒和挫败情绪。

造成航班延误的因素有很多。飞机停场需要在短时间内完成如加油、清洁、配餐等大量工作。如果不能在航班期时刻表规定的起飞时间前做完这些工作，就会发生延误。避免飞机停场延误最简单的方法是航空公司在制定时间表时延长停场时间，以便有足够多的时间来完成所有必要的工作。然而，这将对飞机的有效使用产生很大影响，这意味着航空公司将失去许多旅客偏爱的起飞时间。同时，还需要向机场调度委员会申请新的起飞和降落时间。因此，最好的解决办法是让航空公司采取措施尽量避免延误。对于需要处理自身停机坪服务的航空公司来说，有必要确保其在高峰时期有足够的设备和人员，这意味着增加成本。在安排时间表时避免极端高峰期也是明智而有效的办法。此外，如果员工能够机动灵活地做任何需要做的工作，航空公司就会大大缩短停场时间。然而，这是以支付昂贵的工资为代价的。对于委托服务代理人来完成停机坪服务的航空公司来说，如果有多个代理人可供选择，则确保正点率就比较容易。

如果有旅客未完成办理登机手续，或者办理登机手续时间过晚，没有足够的时间走出登机口，那么航班就会延误。如果旅客的行李没有及时装入货舱，延误也会发生。所有这些问题在理论上都可以用延长航空公司的办理登机时间来缓解。然而，这可能会导致航空公司面临竞争压力，而要求旅客遵守延长的登机手续也有难度。也许另一种有效的方法是雇佣更多的雇员和更多的柜台，但是这种方法昂贵得多，而且在许多机场是不可行的，因为机场分配给每个航空公司的登机柜台的数量有限。如果有可能使旅客登机和行李分拣过程自动化，延误将大大减轻，这也是降低成本的好方法。

恶劣天气对航空公司和旅客来说就是旅行噩梦。雪、雨、雾和风都有可能推迟或彻底取消航班。飞机在浓雾中飞行是困难的，因为能见度降低，特别是对于那些高流量的机场。飞机在强风中起飞或着陆也是危险的。最大的问题是顺风或逆风会影响飞机的整体速度，特别是当速度对于安全起飞或着陆至关重要的时候。就像中纬度水域附近的地区会给飞机带来风的问题一样，这些特征也使得这些地区更容易遭受暴风雪的袭击。冰雪会降低能见度，使跑道湿滑，影响关键设备的运行。雷暴会伴随强风和降雨，降雨会降低能见度。雷暴周围的空气可以增加空气中的湍流，但大多数飞机都配备有防雷的保护装置。

除了上述原因之外，诸如机械或维修问题、空中交通拥堵、机组或飞行员问题、安全问题或强制撤离、航空公司或机场过失、有限的跑道空间和由于其他航班延误引起的涟漪效应等因素都会影响航班的到达和离开计划。

第十八课　劫　　持

劫持可以分为四大类，即受过军事训练的恐怖分子突击队，使用暴力的政治团体，政治避难者，或精神不稳定的人。

所有的劫持都是危险的，因为他们利用我们民主国家中最宝贵的财产——人的生命来迫使政府或机关屈从于他们的要求。

劫持是敲诈的一种形式。传统的敲诈，目标往往是个人，敲诈的原因则是由于他们的财富或地位。而劫持则是随便拿几个不知名的旅客和机组人员作为人质。从高级经理到参加包价旅游的小康之家，整个旅行大众都会受到影响，从而激起了舆论的谴责。每人都担心：劫持可能在自己或自己的家族身上发生。

有一次，国际空运协会的一位主任宣称，如果各国政府愿意的话，劫持明天就可制止，但是在我们把防止劫持和对劫持采取行动的责任推给国家之前，我们要对有些航空公司为补充地方当局的保安措施所研订的程序加以研究。这些航空公司有的使用所谓空中警官或武装保安人员，有时在每个航班上使用，有时只在通常来往于敏感地区而需要高度安保措施的航班上使用。有些航空公司使用这种人员是与国家公安局或保安队合作进行的，有些航空公司则主动雇佣并训练他们自己的保安人员。

除了空中警官外，航空公司还在研究其他防止劫持的办法，如机组训练和使用特殊设计的驾驶舱进出口。以色列航空公司在这方面可能处于领先地位，但可以理解的是，它们的做法极端机密。

机场当局也与防止劫持极有关系。事实上国际民航组织的航空保安建议（包括在国际民航组织 17 号附件中）即强调了机场保安的重要性。

目前，机场保安所使用的六种主要技术方法如下。

（1）X 射线甄别行李。

（2）探测金属的门框。

（3）炸药探测器。

（4）心理探测法。

（5）设置隔离区。

（6）使用警犬。

在这些机场防范方法中没有一种是完全有效的，正如 1983—1984 年的几起劫持情况证明，大多数的劫机事件都发生在配备现代化装置的机场。

现在我们来看相关政府是如何对付劫机的。

遇到被劫持的飞机时，政府基本上采用以下三种方法。

（1）拒绝该飞机进入领空或在本国着陆，从而把问题转移给其他国家。

（2）通过谈判的方式使劫持者释放人质并最终使劫持者投降。

（3）使用特种警察或军队猛攻被劫持飞机。

国际民航组织航空保安计划的主要目标则是首先要设法拒绝犯罪者进入飞机以保证旅客的安全。

有了这个目标，国际民航组织认为最重要的因素是检查和甄别旅客及其行李，因此，它的第一行动即是国际民航组织的每个缔约国要制订一个航空保安计划。

国际民航组织附件 17（保安措施）规定缔约国应采取的基本行动如下。

（1）与其他国家和国际民航组织合作，交换和提供有关航空保安的情报。

（2）用搜索和甄别的程序，防止未经批准携带武器和炸药进入飞机。

（3）将机场的飞行区与其他地区隔开并处于监视之下。

（4）要求本国的航空公司采用保安程序。

（5）在处理被劫持的飞机时，将全部有关情报发给所有飞越的和目的地的国家。

（6）对被劫持飞机的旅客和机组采取安全的措施，直到他们的航程结束。

References

[1] U.S. Department of Transportation Federal Aviation Administration. Airplane Flying Handbook[R/OL]. [2013-07-22]. http://www.faa.gov/regulations policies/handdbooks_manuals/aircraft/airplane_handbook/media/faa-h-8083-3b.pdf.

[2] U.S. Department of Transportation Federal Aviation Administration. Aeronautical Information Manual[EB/OL]. [2013-08-22]. Europe Comparison of ATM-Related Operational Performance 2010. http://www.faa.gov/air_traffic/publications/.

[3] Airbus Industry. A320 Flight Operation Manual[R/OL]. [2013-08-10]. http://www.Cockpitseeker.com/wp-content/uploads/A320/pdf/Print Only/PTM%20with%20airbus%20doc/pdf/U0S2SP0-L.pdf.

[4] Anon. Airport and Navigational Lighting System Aids[EB/OL]. [2013-07-20]. http://www. Dauntless-soft.com/products/libarary/books/flt/chapter 14.

[5] Anon. Boeing Company 777 Flight Crew Operations Manual-737NG.co.uk[R/OL]. [2013-07-24]. http:/www.737ng.co.uk/B777%20Flight%20Crew%20Operating%20Manual.

[6] U.S. Department of Transportation Federal Aviation Administration. Digital Terminal Procedures[R/OL].[2013-05-27].http://aeronav.faa.gov/digital_tpp.asp?ver=1004&eff=04-08-2010 & end = 05-06-2010.

[7] International Civil Aviation Organization Radio Navigation Aids[M/OL]. 5th ed. (1996-07-01)[2013-08-12].http://www.ihs.com/products/industry-standards/org/icao/historical/page8.aspx.

[8] International Civil Aviation Organization. 9432-2007 Manual of radiotelephony [R/OL]. 4th ed. [2013-07-27]. http://www.freetd.us/soft2/605888.htm.

[9] U.S. Department of Transportation. Weight and Balance, Handbook 2007[M/OL]. [2013-08-11]. http://www.faa.gov/regulations policies/handbooks manuals/aircraft/media/FAA-H-8083-1A.pdf.

[10] 教育部高等教育司．大学英语课程教学要求[M]．北京：外语教学与研究出版社，2004.

[11] 吴土星．无线电陆空通话教程[M]．北京：中国民航出版社，2008.

[12] 李玉梅．中国民航飞行人员英语阅读教程[M]．北京：中国民航出版社，1997.

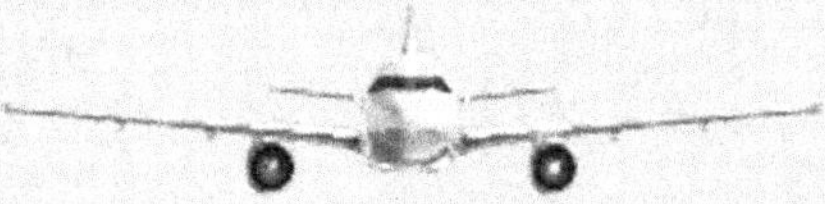

Appendix I

Aviation English Extended Vocabulary

一、爆炸物威胁

anonymous call	匿名电话
emergency evacuation	紧急撤离
escape chute(emergency slides)	逃生滑梯
the bomb disposal squad	拆弹人员
explode	爆炸
flame	火焰、燃烧
explosion	爆炸物
hand grenade	手榴弹
threaten	威胁
terrorist	恐怖分子
hostage	人质
compromise	妥协
forced landing	迫降
burst	爆胎
bank the aircraft	倾斜（压坡度）
stall	失速
jetway	廊桥（美）
air bridge/loading bridge	廊桥（英）
passenger gate	登机口
terminal	候机楼
ground handling	地勤
conveyor	输送带
servicing truck	地面特种车辆
airport passengerbus/ferry	摆渡车
shuttle bus	摆渡车
tug/towing tractor	拖车
tow bar	拖把
ground power unit	地面电源车
air steps	机载客梯
fire engine	消防车
ambulance	救护车
crash tender	事故处理车
wheelbarrow	独轮手推车

security van	保安运货车
ice-melter	除冰车
coach	大客车
refueller	加油车
hydrant dispenser	管线加油车
terrorism attack	恐怖袭击

二、操纵系统故障

flight control system	飞行操纵系统
control system inoperative	操纵系统故障
system jammed	系统卡阻
crank	曲柄（摇把）
thrust reverser	反推，反喷装置
manual controls	人工操纵系统
handles	操纵手柄
switch	开关
stick/column	驾驶杆/驾驶盘
the elevator controls	升降舵操纵系统
the autopilot control system	自动驾驶操纵系统
rudder	方向舵
elevator	升降舵
boosted control	助力系统
knobs	按钮或旋钮
smooth	平稳
the control surface	操纵面
aileron	副翼
slat	缝翼
flap	襟翼
spoiler	扰流板
a flapless landing	无襟翼落地
flap setting	襟翼位置选定（放形态）
the full flap position	全襟翼位置
retract the flaps	收襟翼（收形态）
brakes are unreliable	刹车不可靠
the control stand	操纵台
the pedestal panel	中央操纵台
the rudder bar	方向舵连杆

the flap controls	仅以操纵系统
steering wheel	转向方向盘（前轮）
airbrakes	减速板
flap angle	襟翼角度
pitch trim	俯仰配平
glare shield panel	防眩板
autothrottle system	自动油门系统
autothrust system	自动推力系统（注意两者区别）
bank	坡度倾斜
turn	旋转转弯
climb	爬升
dive	下沉
pressure sensor	压力传感器
accelerometer	加速度计
trim indicator	配平指示器
shed	脱落
instrument landing system	仪表着陆系统
microwave landing system	微波着陆系统
trousers	整流罩
Port—starboard	左舷——右舷

三、电力系统故障

electric failure	供电失效
DC generator	直流发电机
AC generator	交流发电机
APU	辅助电源装置
Wire	电线
circuit breaker	断路器
tripped circuitbreaker	跳闸断开关
loose connection	接触不良
the battery isdown/flat	电瓶电力不足
power supply	电源
reset	复位
power failure shortly	瞬时断电
voltmeter	电压表
fuse	保险丝
blown out fuse	触断保险丝

lead	连线；引线、铅
the bus bar	汇流条
warning flags/light	警告标志/灯
disconnect	断开
short circuit	短路
rectifier	整流器

四、发动机故障

engine failure	发动机失效
engine trouble	发动机故障
engine flame out	发动机熄火
engine shut down	发动机停车
engine feathered	发动机顺浆
engine surge	发动机喘振
engine runs rough	发动机工作不平稳
engine runs smoothly	发动机工作平稳
overheat	超温
engine on fire	发动机起火
engine partially disintegrated	发动机部分爆炸
pod	吊舱
nacelle	吊舱
fan	风扇
LP and HP compressor	低压和高压压缩机
nozzle	喷嘴
engine setting	发动机配置
set the engine toidle	将发动机置于慢车
disintegrate	分裂、爆炸
engine is low on power	发动机马力低
loud thump	很大的响声
vibration	抖震，震动
low rumble	发动机发出低沉的响声
loud bangs	发动机放炮
bird ingestion	吸入飞鸟
warning light flashing on	告警灯闪烁
boost pump	增压泵
cowl	（引擎等的）整流罩
spinner	整流罩

discharging	正在灭火
fire service assistance	消防救援
air inlet or intake	进气道
fan blade	风扇叶片
compressor blade	压缩机叶片
exhaust section	排气部分
the RPM	发动机转数
throttle up/down	加/减油门
trouble-shooting	排除故障
fluctuate	（仪表指示）摆动

五、除/防冰系统故障

anti-icing system inoperative	防冰系统故障
de-icing system inoperative	除冰系统故障
the freezing level	结冰层
icing	结冰
freezing rain	冻雨
anti-icing fluid	防冻液
flushing toilet	冲水厕所
icing indicator	结冰指示器
icing rate indicator	结冰速度指示器
anti-icing duct	防冰导管；防冰装置导管
anti-icing air regulator	防冰空气调节器
pneumatic impulseice-protection system	气动启动脉冲防冰系统
anti-icing valve	防冰装置或门
pitot de-icer	全静压管除冰装置；空速管防冰器

六、风挡问题

windscreen	（英）风挡
windshield	（美）风挡
windshield problem	风挡问题
windshield is icedover	风挡完全结冰
outer windshield crazed	外层风挡破碎
inner windshield	内层风挡
wiper	雨刮器
bird strike	鸟击
smash	击碎
crack	裂纹

transverse crack	横向裂纹
shatter	粉碎性的破裂
unknown foreign object	不明外来物
thump	重击声
decompression	失压
oxygen masks	氧气面罩
request medical assistance	请求医疗援助
request fire service sand first-aid	请求消防和急救

七、空中失火

pilot'scabin	驾驶舱
passenger cabin	客舱
rear cabin	后舱
toilet(restroom)	卫生间
baggage hold	行李舱
fire warning(alarm)	火警
cargo compartment	货仓
extinguisher	灭火器
evacuation	撤离，疏散
open flame	明火
emergency slides/escape chutes	逃生滑梯
fire engine	消防车
fire brigade/firemen	消防队/员
firefighting equipment	灭火设施
asphyxia/suffocate	窒息
engine bleed airsystem	发动机引起系统

The rear aisle carpetis on fire, someone set fire to the petrol in a can.
客舱后部过道地毯着火，有人点燃了罐子里的汽油。

八、劫持

hijack	劫持
intimidate/threaten	威胁
compel/force	强迫
terrorist	恐怖分子
terrorism	恐怖主义
hostage	人质
compromise	妥协
scheduled flight	定期航班

non-scheduled flight	非定期航班
outbound flight	出港航班
inbound flight	进港航班
domestic flight	国内航班
international flight	国际航班
extra section flight	加班飞行
charter flight	包机飞行
passenger flight	客运飞行
cargo flight	货运飞行
business flight	公务飞行
special flight, stateflight	专机
general aviation	通用航空
flight dispatcher	飞行签派员
transit passenger	过站旅客
pilot-in-command	责任机长
flight crew	飞行机组
cabin crew	乘务机组
stewardess	女乘务员
purser	乘务长
ramp commander, rampcontroller	现场指挥员
conquered/subjugated/overcome	制服

九、雷达失效

primary surveillance radar (PSR)	一次监视雷达
precision approach radar (PAR)	精密进近雷达
secondary surveillance radar (SSR)	二次监视雷达
airport surveillance radar (ASR)	场面监视雷达
radar position indication (RPI)	雷达位置指示
radar position symbol(RPS)	雷达位置符号
PSR blip	一次监视雷达回波
SSR response	二次监视雷达应答
radar separation/non-radar separation	雷达间隔/非雷达间隔
aircraft proximity	航空器接近
radar clutter	雷达干扰
radar contact	雷达看到
identified	雷达识别
(compulsory)reporting point	（强制）报告点

significant point	重要点
way point(for RNAV)	航路点

十、起落架故障

undercarriage trouble	起落架故障
landing gear	起落架
gear locked	起落架锁定
the wheel door	轮舱门
burst	爆破（轮胎）
extend/retract thegear	放/收起落架
crank the gear down	人工放下起落架
appear down/up	看上去已放下/收上
jar the wheel down	将轮子震动放下
collapsed	折断
spray	喷洒
belly landing	机腹着陆
gear up landing	收起落架着陆
foam carpet	泡沫毯
gear check	检查起落架
jam	卡阻
low pass	低空通场
the nose wheel	前轮
the wheel well	轮舱
a flat(deflated) tyre	放了气的轮胎
puncture	刺破
emergency extension system	紧急放下系统
the gear is jammed	起落架卡组
does not appear down/up	看上去未放下/收上
touch and go	连续起落，触地拉升
fuel dumping	放油
divert	改航
sort out	解决（问题）

Appendix II

Abbreviations for Aviation English

ADS 自动相关监视　（Automatic dependent surveillance）
AFIS 机场飞行情报服务　（Aerodrome flight information service）
AIS 航行情报服务　（Aeronautical information service）
AMSL 距平均海平面高度　（Above mean sea level）
AOR 责任区　（Area of responsibility）
ATC 空中交通管制　（Air traffic control）
ATD 实际离场时间　（Actual time of departure）
ATIS*自动终端情报服务　（Automatic terminal information service）
ATS 空中交通服务　（Air traffic service）
ATZ 机场交通地带　（Aerodrome traffic zone）
*CAVOK 天气良好　（Ceiling and Visibility OK, i.e. Visibility, cloud and present weather better than prescribed values or condition）
CPDLC 空中交通管制员航空器驾驶员数据链通信　（Controller-pilot data link communications）
CTR 管制地带　（Control zone）
DME 测距器　（Distance measuring equipment）
EET 预计经过时间　（Estimated elapsed time）
ETA 预计到达时间　（Estimated time of arrival or estimating arrival）
ETD 预计离场时间　（Estimated time of departure or estimating departure）
FIC 飞行情报中心　（Flight information center）
FIR 飞行情报区　（Flight information region）
FIS 飞行情报服务　（Flight information service）
HF 高频　（High frequency）
H24 24 小时服务　（Continues day and night service）
IFR 仪表飞行规则　（Instrument flight rules）
ILS 仪表着陆系统　（Instrument landing system）
IMC 仪表气象条件　（Instrument meteorological condition）
*INFO 情报　（Information）
INS 惯性导航系统　（Inertial navigation system）
*MET 气象　（Meteorological or meteorology）
MLS 微波着陆系统　（Microwave landing system）
MNPS 最低导航性能规范　（Minimum navigation performance specifications）
NDB 无方向性信标台　（Non-directional radio beacon）
NOZ 正常运行区　（Normal operating zone）
NTZ 非侵入区　（No-transgression zone）

*NIL 无或无可发送	（None or I have nothing to send you）
*NOTAM 航行通告	（Notice to Airman, i.e. A notice containing information concerning the establishment, condition or change in any aeronautical facility, service procedure or hazard, the timely knowledge of which is essential to personnel concerned with flight operations）
PAOAS 平行进近障碍物评估面	（Parallel approach obstacle assessment surfaces）
QFE 场压	（Atmospheric pressure at aerodrome elevation, or at runway threshold）
QNH 修正海平面气压	（Altimeter sub-scale setting to obtain elevation when on the ground）
RCC 援救协调中心	（Rescue co-ordination center）
*RNAV 区域导航	（Area navigation）
RNP 所需导航性能	（Required navigation performance）
RVSM 缩小垂直间隔	（Reduced vertical separation minimum）
*SELCAL 选择呼叫	（A system which permits the selective calling of individual aircraft over radiotelephone channels linking a ground station with the aircraft）
*SID 标准仪表离场	（Standard instrument departure）
SIGMET*航路重要天气报	（Information concerning en-route weather phenomena which may affect safety of aircraft operations）
SNOWTAM*雪情通告	（A special series NOTAM notifying the presence or removal of hazardous conditions due to snow, ice, slush or standing water associated with snow, slush and ice on the movement area, by means of a special format）
*SPECIAL 特选报	（Special meteorological report）
SSR 二次监视雷达	（Secondary surveillance radar）
SST 超音速运输机	（Supersonic transport）
*STAR 标准仪表进场	（Standard terminal arrival route）
TCAS 或 ACAS*机载防撞系统	（Traffic alert and collision avoidance system/Airborne collision avoidance system）
*TAF 机场预报	（Aerodrome forecast）
TMA 终端管制区	（Terminal control area）
UHF 特高频	（Ultra-high frequency）
UIR 高空情报区	（Upper flight information region）
UTC 协调世界时	（Coordinated universal time）
*VASIS 目视进近坡度指示系统	（Visual approach slope indicator system）

VFR 目视飞行规则 （Visual flight rules）
VHF 甚高频 （Very high frequency）
VIP 要客 （Very important person）
VMC 目视气象条件 （Visual meteorological conditions）
VOLMET*对空天气广播 （Meteorological information for aircraft in flight）
VOR 全向信标台 （VHF omnidirectional radio range）
ATC 空中交通管制员 （Air traffic controller）
*ATIS 自动终端信息服务 （Automatical terminal information service)
AIDS 自动数据交换系统 （Automatic Data Interchange System)
ACARS 飞机通信寻址和报告系统（aircraft communication Addressing and reporting system）
CAAC 中国民用航空局 （Civil Aviation Administration of China）
*CRM 机组资源管理 （Crew resource management）
*CG 重心 （Center of gravity）
CAVOK 云高和能见度好 （Cloud and visibility ok）
DME 测距仪 （Distance measuring equipment）
*EFIS 电子飞行仪表系统 （Electrical flight instrument system）
ECAM 电子中央飞行监控器 （Electrical centralized aircraft monitor）
ETD 预计离场时间 （Estimated time of departure）
ETA 预计到达时间 （Estimated time of arrival）
ETO 预计飞越时间 （Estimated time of over）
EWD 发动机警告显示 （Engine warning display）
FMC 飞行管理计算机 （Flight management computer）
*FOM 航行手册 （Flight operation manuls）
*FOB 机上燃油 （Fuel on board）
*GPS 全球定位系统 （Global positioning system）
*GPWS 近地警告系统 （Ground proximity warning system）
HIS 危害情报系统，危险信息系统（Hazard Information System）
ILS 仪表着陆系统 （Instrument landing system）
ICAO 国际民航组织 （International Civil Aviation Organization）
IFR 仪表飞行规则 （Instrument flight rules）
IGS 仪表引导系统 （Instrument guidance system）
*MEL 最低设备清单 （Minimum equipment list）
MFD 多功能显示器 （Multi-functional display）
MCDU 多功能控制组件 （Multi function control display unit）
*ND 导航显示 （Navigation display）
NDB 无方向信标台 （Non-directional Beacon）
OPI 口语能力面试 （Oral Proficiency interview）

PEPEC 中国飞行员英语能力测试（Pilot English Proficiency Examination of China）
*PFD 主飞行显示（Primary flight display）
*PA 乘客广播（Passenger address）
*POB 机上乘客（Passenger on board）
*QRH 快速检查手册（Quick reference handbook）
RVR 跑道视程（Runway visual range）.
RVSM 缩小最小垂直间隔（Reduce vertical separation minimum）
*RA 决断咨询（Resolution advisory）
SID 标准离场程序（Standard instrument departure）
*SOP 标准操作程序（Standard operating procedure）
*TCAS 空中警告防撞系统（Traffic alert and collision avoidance system）
*TA 交通警告（Traffic alert）
VFR 目视飞行规则（Visual flight rules）
VOR 甚高频全向信标台（VHF Omnidirection Range）

注：以上缩略语通常按照字母连续读出，而不按照特殊的发音方法发音。标有*号的缩略语可作为一个单词，按照英语发音规则发音。